D1521112

Portrayals of Children in Popular Culture

Portrayals of Children in Popular Culture

Fleeting Images

Edited by
Vibiana Bowman Cvetkovic
Debbie Olson

LEXINGTON BOOKS
Lanham • Boulder • New York • Toronto • Plymouth, UK

Published by Lexington Books
A wholly owned subsidiary of The Rowman & Littlefield Publishing Group, Inc.
4501 Forbes Boulevard, Suite 200, Lanham, Maryland 20706
www.rowman.com

10 Thornbury Road, Plymouth PL6 7PP, United Kingdom

Copyright © 2013 by Lexington Books

British Library Cataloguing in Publication Information Available

Library of Congress Cataloging-in-Publication Data
Library of Congress Cataloguing-in-Publication Data Available
ISBN 978-0-7391-6748-9 (cloth : alk. paper)—ISBN 978-0-7391-7956-7 (electronic)

♾™ The paper used in this publication meets the minimum requirements of American National Standard for Information Sciences—Permanence of Paper for Printed Library Materials, ANSI/NISO Z39.48-1992.

Printed in the United States of America

Dedications

This is dedicated to the ones I love: Liz, Tatiana, Anna, Natasha, Michael, David (the offspring); and to my wonderful husband, Nick. (VBC)

"To succeed you have to believe in something with such a passion that it becomes a reality" (Anita Roddick). I'd like to thank my Dad, my best boys, Rick and Justin, and my husband Curt for helping me turn my passion into a reality. (DO)

Contents

About This Book
Vibiana Bowman Cvetkovic and Debbie Olson

> Some say that as we grow up, we become different people at different ages, but I don't believe this. I think we remain the same throughout, merely passing in these years from one room, to another, but always in the same house. If we unlock the rooms of the far past, we can look in and see ourselves beginning to become you and me.
>
> James M. Barrie, *Peter Pan* (1905)

Fleeting Images: Portrayals of Children in Popular Culture is a collection of essays which examine images of "children" and "childhood" in popular culture—in print, online, on television shows, and in films. The terms are in quotes to indicate that, for the most part, in these essays, it is the *constructions* of "children" and "childhood" rather than actual *children* or actual *childhoods* which are explored. In the chapters that *are* concerned with depictions of actual, individual children (such as in Anderson's chapter on YouTube and Nardella's chapter on pageant queens, gymnasts, and skaters), the authors explore how the images of those children conform or "trouble" current notions of what it means to be a child engaged in a contemporary "childhood." The work of the scholars represented in this collection is unique because of the academic discourse which is employed—that of "Childhood Studies." Childhood Studies is a relative newcomer to the academy. While there have been Childhood Studies programs in Europe since the 1980s, at present there is only one Childhood Studies PhD program in North America (Rutgers, The State University, Camden, New Jersey).[1] As such, it is necessary to situate the works in this collection with regard to this new field; specifically the particular perspective utilized by the authors and their interdisciplinary approach.

An interdisciplinary approach is one which draws upon various academic fields—their methodologies, theoretical approaches, and scholarly conventions—for scholarly research.[2] "Interdisciplines," such as Women's Studies, African American Studies and Popular Culture studies are a product of the twentieth century. For example, one of the first interdisciplines, "American Studies," came into being in the first decades of the twentieth century. After World War II, American Studies programs were funded by Carnegie Corporation at prestigious universities such as Brown, Amherst, Minnesota, and the University of Pennsylvania.[3] As the second half of the twentieth century advanced so did interdisciplines. They arose from social and political movements; examples include such areas as Women's Studies, African American Studies, and LGBT Studies. Childhood Studies can thus be viewed as the most recent entry in the progressive academic endeavor to represent hitherto unrepresented voices, political stances, and non-hegemenous points of view. The approach of Childhood Studies can best be characterized by a term coined by Daniel Cook: "pediocularity."[4]

Cook defines pediocularity as "seeing with children's eyes . . . for decentering the adult view and centering that of the child."[5] While Cook uses the term in *The Commodification of Childhood* specifically with regard to marketing practices regarding the material culture of childhood in the first half of the twentieth century, the term is also useful for characterizing an academic approach which "decenters" the adult and privileges the child. In this collection the scholars have all placed "childhood" front and center.

Fleeting Images is divided into three parts: part One examines images of children in print and online sources; part Two looks at children as featured on television; and part Three studies children in film. The editors acknowledge that there is an arbitrariness in the categories particularly from the vantage point of the first part of the twenty-first century where lines between types of media are increasingly blurred. Many of the essays included in this collection were previously published. A majority appeared in *Red Feather: An International Journal of Children's Visual Culture* (Murphy, Gennaro, Blue, Chappell, Shepard, Linder, and Casaregola). The essay by Olson was published in *MP: An Online Feminist Journal*. These works are included in *Fleeting Images* with permission from those journals. The essays by Franzini, Anderson, Nardella, Lee, Abate, Fink, and Dong appear in print for the first time in this collection. The backgrounds and expertise of the authors represented in this collection are richly diverse, as are their methods and styles. The stylistic differences have been preserved in order to best represent the voices and approaches of the various authors.

In part One, Murphy and Franzini examine portrayals of childhood and girlhood in popular magazines. Murphy interrogates the concept of "Girl Power" as a marketing tool utilized by magazines aimed at young women such as *CosmoGirl*, *Teen Elle*, and *Teen Vogue*. Franzini investigates the parenting advice given in one of the most well-known and well-respected magazines devoted to the topic, *Parents*. Specifically, Franzini looks at the construction of contemporary childhood invoked by the authors of the magazine's recommendations columns for parents regarding appropriate media for children of varying ages. Gennaro explores the Abercrombie & Fitch advertising controversies. A & F has come under fire in the popular press for its provocative imagery in its advertising campaigns—imagery known for both its sensuality and use of seemingly teenaged models. Controversies surrounding the portrayal of children also exist in new media such as the incredibly successful Internet venture, YouTube, which—as its slogan announces—allows individuals to "broadcast" themselves. Anderson looks at the history of parent-made films, from home movies to YouTube. She explores how technology has shifted cultural perspectives of public versus private ("protected") childhoods.

The stories of post World War II childhood and the rise of television are intertwined. From the baby boomers (the first generation to grow up with television friends), to the paradigm shift in children's programming brought about by the debut of *Sesame Street*, to the rise of niche programming via cable TV, children's relationship with and portrayal on television has been an object of intense scrutiny and public debate. In part Two, the authors explore some of those controversies and some of those relationships. Nardella examines the pursuit of ideal beauty with regard to the girl child. She looks at reality TV (*Toddlers and Tiaras*) and female dominated sports events such as gymnastics and ice skating. Nardella is particularly interested in the importance given to the imagery of teeth and puts this into conversation with the focus on teeth and youthful beauty in Barrie's *Peter Pan*. Blue also looks at visual portrayals of children but that of the fictionalized children that appear in *Law & Order: Special Victims Unit*. She explores what she terms, the "multiple" and "contradictory" ways that children function in the show. Lee and Chappell examine two different educational shows, *Pororo* (a production of the Korean Educational Broadcast System) and *Dora the Explorer* (Nick Jr.), from a multicultural perspective. Lee looks at how the cultural values of Korean society regarding childhood are transmitted/reflected in a book series based on its most popular children's shows. Chappell states that *Dora* also transmits "specific ideologies regarding childhood and society." Chappell situates the show with regard to current political debates regarding immigration and controversies about America's increasing multiculturalism. The author also discusses how *Dora* folds its child viewer's familiarity with new technologies and expectations of interactivity into its story lines.

Films for and about children have been a staple of the industry throughout the past 100 plus years. One of the first feature films, an action/adventure story starring D. W. Griffith, was *Rescued from the Eagle's Nest* (Edison Studios, 1908). The story revolved around how a heroic pioneer father saves his baby daughter from a predatory eagle. What does the child mean to, and in, cinema? As Karen Lury suggests, children in film seem to "prefer the messiness, the ambivalent relations, confusing associations and excitable passions that are allowed in childhood" and find unique visual expression in the cinema. The portrayal of innocence idealized, or fractured and challenged, continually draws adult audiences to relive their own childhoods onscreen.[6] Images of children, consumed by both adults and children, function in richly textured ways on the silver screen. As Patricia Holland explains the significance of any single picture or visual representation is never complete,"[7] and the critical examination of the cinematic child is particularly significant as "children have been the object of imagery, [but] very rarely its makers."[8] In part Three the contributor's examine this relationship between children and cinema, exploring how children and childhood are portrayed and utilized in films. Abate, Shepard, and Olson turn a critical eye towards contemporary children's films. Abate examines *Where the Wild Things Are*, the 2009 film and the classic Sendak picture book. She explores how each work troubles the Romantic notion of childhood and confronts the specter of nostalgia for adults of childhood lost. Shepard discusses the anthropomorphized antagonists in the long strong of commercially successful Pixar films in terms of children's feelings of empowerment and marginalization. Olson blends marketing and visual culture theory to critique the use of color in the films of Tim Burton. Olson pays particular attention to Burton's color palette with regard to the merchandising of film-related products to children. Fink, Dong, and Linder look at the cultural, political, and societal milieus which shaped films that feature children and their childhoods in post World War II England, the war-torn Middle East, and a racially divided America. Casaregola reads the classic film, *Meet Me in St. Louis*, from a child-centric perspective and examines questions of childhood innocence and nostalgia for an imagined golden age and time.

Together, the essays in this collection interrogate classic notions of childhood innocence, knowledge, agency, and the fluid position of the signifier "child" within contemporary media forms. The interdisciplinary works in this collection function as a testament to the infectiousness of the child image in print, television, and cinematic contexts. The editors wish to thank the authors for their contributions to this timely and compelling collection. The essays here represent a new avenue of discursive scholarship; the questions raised and connections made provide fresh insights and unique perspectives to topics regarding children and childhood and their representation within multiple media platforms. The growing field of Childhood Studies is enriched by the intellectual originality represented by this volume's authors. We hope our readers will be inspired to view more critically and ask new questions about the enduring and captivating image of the child.

Notes

1. For more detailed information about the history of Childhood Studies see Vibiana Bowman and Laura B. Spencer, "Toward a Definition of Children and Childhood Studies in *Scholarly Resources for Children and Childhood Studies: A Research Guide and Annotated Bibliography* edited by Vibiana Bowman (Lanham, MD: Scarecrow Press, 2007), 3- 16. Also, Mary Jane Kehily, "Understanding Childhood: An Introduction to Some Key Themes and Issues," in An Introduction to Childhood Studies edited by Mary Jane Kehily (Maidenhead, UK: Open University Press, 2004), 1-21.

2. Bowman, "Toward," *Scholarly*, 6.

3. For an in-depth history of interdisciplinary studies see Julie Thompson Klein's *Interdisciplinarity: History, Theory, and Practice* (Detroit, MI: Wayne State University Press, 1990).

4. Daniel T. Cook, "Pediocularity: From The Child's Point of View," in The *Commodification of Childhood: The Children's Clothing Industry and the Rise of the Child Consumer* (Durham: Duke University Press, 2004), 66-95.

5. Cook, "Pediocularity," *Commodification*, 67.

6. Karen Lury, *The Child in Film: Tears, Fears, and Fairytales*. New Brunswick: Rutgers, UP. 2010. 5.

7. Patricia Holland. *Picturing Childhood: The Myth of the Child in Popular Memory*. New York: L.B. Tauris, 2004. 5.

8. Holland, 20.

Part One
Print and the Web

Chapter One
"The Girl You've Always Wanted to Be!"
Girl Power and Commodity Postfeminism
in Teen Magazines
by Caryn Murphy

Introduction

In 2003, a print industry executive told *Advertising Age* that he characterized the new entrants in the teen girls' magazine market according to long-established types. The optimism and energy of *CosmoGirl* positioned it as "the cheerleader," in contrast to "the prom queen" post held by fashion-focused *Teen Vogue* and the "student council president" designation belonging to *Elle Girl*, the most diverse and inclusive of these titles.[1] The executive did not include *Teen People*, the magazine that launched the sibling publication trend in 1998, but its emphasis on celebrities would no doubt pigeonhole it as the class gossip. All of these magazines were introduced in the late 1990s and early 2000s, with the aim of securing advertising dollars directed at the notably large youth demographic, often referred to as "Generation Y."[2] These titles positioned themselves as alternative to stalwarts *YM*, *Teen*, and the long-standing industry leader, *Seventeen*. As is evident in the executive's observations, however, their approach to young femininity did not offer a legitimately "new" address to young women, but instead targeted Generation Y with representations of idealized girlhood that easily fit into recognizable cultural norms and expectations.

The industrial trend of teen-targeted iterations of long-established magazines is unusual because it emerged as print publications were in decline due to competition from web-based content. By 2006, most of these magazines had shuttered or retreated to online-only versions, but for nearly a decade they battled over the large, valuable teen girl market segment.[3] Through their intense proliferation, teen magazines became an important site of negotiation within the larger mediated discourse of girl power that circulated during this time. Articles, features, and advertisements in magazines targeted towards a teen girl reader-ship assume that girls already possess the girl power characteristics of independ-ence, strength, and ability, but they offer "choices" in terms of how to express those characteristics outwardly, creating "work" associated with expressing girl power as both self-reliance and traditional feminine beauty. Despite the claims of the executive quoted above, there is little differentiation in teen girls' maga-zines; they emphasize fashion, celebrity culture, and health and beauty products. The central "commodity" is the teen girl readership itself, which is sold by mag-azine publishers to the plethora of advertisers who seek to gain the attention of this demographic.

The cultural identity of Generation Y is inextricably linked with girl power, a discourse of youth and femininity that circulated meaningfully, beginning in the mid-1990s. Barbara Hudson has argued that the traditional discourses of femininity and adolescence are at odds with each other; cultural expectations have supported feminine passivity and dependence, and girls who display youth-ful aggression and ambition are disparaged as overly masculine.[4] Girl power addressed this contradiction by associating youthful femininity with self-reliance, confidence, and athleticism. Although the "girl power" phrase became particularly associated with popular music (the Spice Girls, a globally successful pop group from the UK, employed it as a mantra), part of its resonance derived from its function as a response to cultural fears about girls' development. Suc-cessful books including Mary Pipher's *Reviving Ophelia* and Peggy Orenstein's *Schoolgirls* drew mainstream attention to a "confidence gap" between girls and boys that emerged at the onset of adolescence.[5] In her overview of the girl power discourse, Emilie Zaslow argues that the concerns about girls' development ex-pressed in these studies helped to shift the dynamics of how young women were positioned in and by the larger media culture. Other major influences include third wave feminism, which in turn was informed by the grassroots riot grrrl movement, and the cultural backlash against the gains of second wave femi-nism.[6] Girl power has been critiqued extensively by cultural commentators who view it as a cynical attempt to market consumer goods to young women.[7] How-ever, at least part of the impetus behind girl power is a desire to free young girls from the strictures of traditional femininity that were associated with a loss of self-esteem in adolescence. The commodification of this desire is a process on display in the late 1990s proliferation of teen girls' magazines.

Although the discourse is informed by feminist movements, Jessica K. Taft has argued that the postfeminist signification of girl power has circulated more forcefully. Postfeminism itself is a contested concept, but it generally refers to the cultural circumstance in which feminism has become irrelevant or unneces-sary. In her detailed taxonomy, Sarah Projansky offers "equality and choice postfeminism" as a category of representations focused on the supposed success of feminism in attaining gender equity, and increasing the availability of choices for women. It asserts that feminism is no longer necessary because it has succeeded.[8] This category resonates with Taft's examination of girl power as a post-feminist discourse.[9] Girl power has been used to assert that structural inequality either no longer exists, or is no longer significant. Each individual girl is able to succeed or fail based on her own merits, and this is presented as though choices and opportunities are equally available to all young women, regardless of race, class, or sexuality. Projansky argues that equality and choice postfeminism positions women as social, political, and economic equals whose primary struggles involve navigating the "choice" between obligations related to work and family. In teen girls' magazines, equality and choice postfeminism positions young women as equals who are navigating choices related to self-improvement and identity construction.

"Having It All": Girl Power as Consumer Power

The content of teen girls' magazines is directly shaped by the goals of the advertisers who support their publication. Robert Goldman has argued persuasively that advertisers acknowledged feminism in the late 1980s in order to re-shape its signification; in the pages of women's magazines, a movement towards gender equality became associated with consumer products. Advertising acknowledged feminism in order to associate it with the accoutrements of femininity, a process that resulted in what he terms "commodity feminism." Goldman writes of this trend, "Feminism has been reduced to the status of a mere signifier, so that it may be re-encoded by advertisers as a sequence of visual clichés and reified signifiers."[10] Readers are thus encouraged to purchase a "feminist" identity; they express their equality through their ability to consume. In the teen girls' magazines under examination here, girl power similarly becomes a signifier. Advertisers construct a world in which girls' lives are shaped by equality and choice; they represent young multicultural femininity in terms of beauty, independence, athleticism, and self-assurance, and they ask young women to display these characteristics outwardly through conspicuous consumption. Representations of girls' empowerment in magazine advertising illuminate how the feminist potential of the girl power discourse ultimately becomes muted and redirected towards consumer activism and the construction of individual identity.

Although girl power rejects feminine passivity, advertisers have used it to reinforce the importance of physical beauty. Teen girls' magazines offer democratic beauty ideals, in which every young woman can be "beautiful" as long as she subscribes to the consumerist notion of beauty supported by advertisers. These magazines demonstrate that beauty is something that can be purchased through specific products and brands, and that it is equally available to all young women (a position which presumes a significant amount of disposable income). This is not a marketing innovation designed for Generation Y; Angela McRobbie, Dawn Currie, and others have noted the centrality of beauty commodification in the address of girls' magazines to their readers.[11] The shift in signification occurs in terms of the ultimate goal of the reader-consumer. In her study of contemporary teen girls' culture in Australia, Susan Hopkins notes that "cosmetics, fashion and beauty commodities used to be marketed with the implicit promise that 'this product will make you loveable.' Today these beauty products are sold with the suggestion 'this will make you powerful.'"[12] Through the process of commodity feminism, advertisers address young women as empowered subjects, and they work to associate the signification of empowerment with specific products. In *The Beauty Myth*, Naomi Wolf argues that if women are truly empowered (as postfeminist culture argues that they are) they should be able to choose whether or not to participate in the trappings of feminine beauty work.[13] Teen girls' magazines work to represent "beauty" as the only healthy, powerful choice.

Advertisements for a wide range of consumer products acknowledge girl power as they simultaneously remove it from any context of girls' social authority and represent it solely in relation to the development and maintenance of physical beauty. In *CosmoGirl*, Bonne Bell cosmetics advertises a powder and concealer combination with a close-up shot of an attractive young white girl and the tagline, "I can face change head on."[14] The advertisement constructs a world in which the only relevant difficulties that young women face can easily be conquered with a clear, glowing complexion. Similarly, Pantene Pro-V shampoo advertises "Curl Power," shifting any association between the girl power phrase and social and cultural authority to a solitary association between "power" and physical beauty.[15]

Commodity feminism is also visible in advertisements that utilize girl power as a signifier and consumer products as direct signifieds. A series of advertisements for Tommy Girl cologne in *CosmoGirl* and other teen magazines proclaimed the scent "A Declaration of Independence."[16] The ads, each featuring an attractive model shot in close-up, incorporated iterations of the American flag, and the Tommy Girl logo in red, white, and blue. The advertisement works to form an association between abstract characteristics of individualism, independence, and patriotism with the commodity, thus making them available for purchase. Pond's Overnight Blemish Reducer addresses readers with the line, "YOU refuse to believe life is about trade-offs," associating the empowered young woman's reluctance to compromise with the purchase of face cream.[17] A 2001 advertisement for Timex shows a young woman in motion and her statement of empowerment: "I wish people would quit telling me I can do anything I want. I never thought I couldn't."[18] These advertisements construct girl power as an already-constituted identity; it becomes empowerment that is so obvious that it is taken for granted, and it finds its key expression through the purchase and display of consumer products.

Susan Faludi has argued that the backlash against second wave feminism particularly demonized adult women for trying to "have it all," meaning having both a fulfilling career and a family life. Features on "infertility epidemics" and the "husband shortage" in popular news and lifestyle publications served as warnings to young women who put off marriage and childbearing to focus on career development.[19] Although the metaphorical notion that girls can "have it all" is present in any number of ads in teen girls' magazines, the phrase makes a literal appearance in an advertisement for Stuff, teen girl superstar Hilary Duff's product line.[20] Within the ad, "having it all" is redefined as having all of the apparel, accessories, and cosmetics to which Duff has lent her name and seal of approval. In other literal associations, concerns about girls' self-esteem become a brand, Self Esteem clothing and accessories, advertised in *YM* with the tagline, "Inspire to Be."[21] Again, the tagline refers to the fact that teen girl shoppers already have high levels of self-esteem, which they express through clothing and accessories. Their role is not to "aspire," but to "inspire" others, and they do this by displaying their commodified, empowered identities.

A smaller number of advertisements represent girl power as action and athleticism, working to associate physical strength with the ability to perform beauty work. An ad for Skechers shoes in *Teen People* draws on the style of classic James Bond movie posters, recasting the central role with a blonde heroine on the run.[22] An ad for pHisoderm face cleanser features a young woman in a martial arts costume, preparing for combat with two giant Q-tips; the complementary tagline, "Kick acne anytime, anywhere," refers to girl power strength and athleticism and re-signifies these traits as related to "battling" blemishes.[23] Frequent advertiser Bonne Bell sponsored a 2003 essay contest for teen girls, asking them to explain how sports have impacted their lives. The "Be Everything You Are" promotion worked to associate the company's cosmetics with girls' athleticism, encouraging girls to embrace multiple identities and deny any distance between the accoutrements of traditional femininity and newer opportunities for social participation.

When *Teen Vogue* debuted in 2003, *USA Today* critiqued the tendency to "hawk fake girl power" in the teen magazine market.[24] Journalist Laura Vanderkam contends that contemporary magazines are different from their predecessors because they do not attempt to sell products by making girls feel unattractive or inadequate. Instead, they flatter young women's sensibilities with repetitive messages of empowerment and self-confidence, and then offer fashion and beauty work as the appropriate outlet for those attributes. Notably, this assessment relies on the assumption that there is such a thing as "authentic" girl power. Vanderkam writes, "Girls deserve real opportunities to explore untamed corners of the world, try new activities that test their physical limits and see how much they're capable of - beyond the confines of the mall."[25] The continual

resignification of girl power as consumer power in teen girls' magazines at-
tempted to fix the discourse, but there was resistance to this limited vision of the
scope of girls' social authority.

"Be Whatever You Decide": Girl Power as Self-Invention

Postfeminism intersects with neoliberalism as both are ideological positions
that separate the individual from social and institutional forces to form an idealized, self-monitoring subject. For Rosalind Gill, "It is clear that the autonomous,
calculating, self-regulating subject of neoliberalism bears a strong resemblance
to the active, freely choosing, self-reinventing subject of postfeminism."[26] In her
study of the development of neoliberal subjectivities, Marnina Gonick argues
that individuals are prompted to surveil themselves in line with "the articulation
of identity as choice and self-determination."[27] Gonick quotes Anthony Giddens
when she writes that the process of individualization "involves an increasing
tendency to self-monitoring, so that 'we are, not what we are, but what we make
of ourselves.'"[28] Features and advertisements in teen girls' magazines encourage
readers to view the construction of identity as a continuous process of becoming
and a limitless opportunity for self-improvement. An article in the August 2001
issue of *CosmoGirl* addresses readers with the headline: "Go Back to School as
the Girl You've Always Wanted to Be!" The brief article offers tips to teen
readers on how they can transform themselves in order to create positive changes in their lives. Advertising is complementary to this kind of editorial copy because advertisers frequently play on readers' desires to transform themselves,
and they suggest specific products to be of use in the effort.

Advertising campaigns in teen girls' magazines including *CosmoGirl, Seventeen, Teen People*, and *YM* frequently utilize girl power as a signifier that represents the ability to define the self. An ad for got2b hairstyling products in *Seventeen* proclaims, "You choose the attitude, we help you create it."[29] Bonne Bell
cosmetics addresses *Teen People* readers with a full-page close-up of a teenage
model and the tagline, "Be whatever you decide. It's beautiful."[30] Readers are
encouraged via the mode of address to see themselves in the ad, which implicitly
flatters the reader's existing characteristics while gently suggesting that choosing to use the cosmetics will help her to communicate her chosen identity with
other people. Secret deodorant advertises three scents (Genuine, Ambition, Optimism) as three different personalities, assuring *CosmoGirl* readers that these
formulas named for abstract characteristics are "Made to match your strength
and individuality" and "They're a sheer expression of you."[31] The three scents
are represented in the ad by separate images of women's feet. "Genuine" is de-
picted as bare feet walking in sand, "Ambition" is a pair of feet in pink, open-

toed high heels, and "Optimism" is represented by a single glass slipper, referencing the Cinderella fairy tale. The Secret ad is an example of commodity feminism; it takes girl power rhetoric of "strength and individuality" and reframes these abstract terms to refer to a strong deodorant and the choice between a limited number of self-defining options. The ad also participates in the neoliberal process of individualization by inviting readers to identify with each of the three "personalities" presented, and to see each of these options as "expressions" of the self.

The Brat catalog and website, offering apparel and accessories for teenage girls, advertises the ability to "Create Your Own Defining Look," along with girl power buzzwords: "Empowerment" and "Individual Style."[32] An unusual ad for Honeycomb cereal features a girl immersed in a pink bathtub full of milk and cereal and the tagline "Anything but ordinary."[33] Within this frame, eating cereal becomes an expression of a unique, boundary-defying feminine personality. Melissa Shoes advertises the ability to express selfhood through footwear with the tagline "Designed by Melissa. Defined by you," in *Seventeen*.[34] Another advertisement for Hilary Duff's Stuff features a "handwritten" note from the star explaining, "I know who I am, but I'm not the same every day . . . Don't just live life, create it."[35]The advertisement encapsulates the relationship between girl power and individualization, as it encourages readers to constantly create expressions of selfhood with consumer goods; having authority is equated with taking control of one's own identity display.

Commodity postfeminism is also visible in the kinds of activism supported by teen girls' magazines. Magazines including *Seventeen* and *CosmoGirl* present features on issues that are of major concern to young women, and these features emphasize individual concerns and personal appearance over collective action and political engagement. Consumer activism is prominent in advertisements for the Candie's Foundation in *Seventeen*; the shoe company extols the virtues of its own public information campaign on teen pregnancy, linking the purchase of shoes with support for the company's interest in the social issue.[36] Missy Elliott advertises Viva Glam from Mac Cosmetics in *Seventeen*, with all proceeds going to support the Mac AIDS Fund.[37] Readers are thus encouraged to participate in social activism by purchasing fashion and beauty products that reaffirm their investment in the project of the self. Teen girls' magazines impede the possibility that girls might use their "power" for collective organization and social change by instead stressing beauty work as a natural outlet for girls' authority.

Multiculturalism as Assimilation
in Girl Power Advertising

Teen girls' magazines offer multicultural representations of young femininity, making no distinction based on race, ethnicity, or socioeconomic class factors and how they might affect the accessibility or attainability of girl power. In
her discussion of equality and choice postfeminism, Sarah Projansky argues that
"postfeminist representations depend on an assimilationist mode of representation to erase race as a legitimate social category for analysis. As a result, 'wom-
en' is meant to stand for all women but does so through the lens of whiteness."[38]
The magazines that target Generation Y offer more racially and ethnically diverse representations than their predecessors, but they continue to privilege
whiteness. The "declaration of independence" promised by Tommy Girl cologne
is framed similarly around a blond, blue-eyed model and an African American
model in separate full-page advertisements. Although Skechers places a white,
athletic heroine at the center of its Bond-style shoe ad, African American and
Asian girls are also posed as action heroines within the frame. An advertisement
for Secret deodorant features an attractive young Indian woman costumed as a
princess and the tagline reads, "When you're strong, you sparkle."[39] The majority of models featured in these magazines are young white women, but young
women of varying racial and ethnic backgrounds are regularly represented with
the same rhetoric of equality and choice that forms the dominant mode of address within their pages. An advertisement for Rajman swimwear in *CosmoGirl*
features a young Asian model cavorting on a beach in a swimsuit. The ad reads:
"This young Betty is," followed by a column of girl power attributes: "sponta-
neous, independent, hyper, street sweet, confident, alternative, global, sharp,
fearless," and "urban."[40] Within the frame of the ad, racial and ethnic identity is
visible but unnamed; the relevance of racial and ethnic identity is denied in favor of a "global" identity that may be claimed by anyone who purchases the
exclusive line of department store swimwear.

Marnina Gonick argues that this type of assimilation displaces social attitudes and structures onto the individual. She writes:

> When girls encounter neoliberal discourse espousing a conviction that
> "anyone who works hard can get ahead' and 'women have made great
> gains towards equality," they are led to understand their own experience of
> successes and failures as a product of their individual effort. How they are
> positioned within the changing cultural, political, economic, and social
> climate insistent on a direct relationship between individualism and indi-
> vidual aspiration does not get factored in.[41]

Assimilationist representations of young femininity deny the relevance of
race and ethnicity as factors of difference that have real material effects in

young women's lives. They represent whiteness as the norm, and they reinforce this by framing young women of other racial and ethnic backgrounds with the same rhetoric of commodified empowerment that is used to create the white norm.

Conclusion

In her recent examination of the connections between grassroots feminism, popular music, and girl power, Marisa Meltzer contends that the hyper-commercialism of young women's empowerment does not necessarily foreclose the liberating possibilities of the discourse. For example, although the Spice Girls offer a mainstream iteration of empowerment rhetoric, they legitimately opened up a space for young female fans to question or resist traditional social expectations of passive femininity.[42] The expansion of the teen girls' magazine market in the late 1990s is evidence of the importance of this demographic to advertisers and to the culture at large. Although I have argued that representations of young femininity have worked to define "girl power" within postfeminist parameters, the existence of differentiation in the market, however slight, also opens up more possibilities for young women to read and identify against the grain that marketers intend.

Teen girls' magazines present girl power as a foregone conclusion, rather than as a possibility for individual girls' empowerment. They address young women as already strong, independent, smart, and pretty, but flood them with messages about how best to employ these attributes for individual advantage. These magazines flatter young women with messages about their social authority and cultural importance, masking not only young women's experience of difference, but also their real factors of dependence. The readership for teen girls' magazines (which often skews younger than the teenage years) are not only economic dependents (depending primarily on their parents for financial support), but also systemic dependents (not yet recognized as full citizens under the law). Teenage girls have different legal rights than adult women, for example; they cannot participate in the political system by voting until they reach age eighteen, and they are legally bound to the educational system. Teen magazines address these young women as autonomous individuals, though they literally do not hold the rights and responsibilities associated with full citizenship.

Susan Hopkins argues that within Australian teen magazines, "Feminist issues become a question of how best to work the system for individual advantage. The assumed girl reader is self-possessed, articulate, aware, cool and confident."[43] Teen magazines in the United States formulate a similar mode of address in which the reader is flattered as already equal within the social system (and sometimes represented as more than equal). Equality is represented as the ability to make choices, and magazines frame the available choices in terms of identity construction and self-improvement. The continuous construction of the self is linked again and again with commodities that contribute to the attainment of physical beauty and the power to create the self as an object. Teen girls' magazines utilize the rhetoric of equality and choice to contain girl power within the realm of patriarchal capitalism, attempting to deny the subversive possibilities of the discourse.

Notes

1. George Janson, identified as the director of print at Mediaedge:cia, is quoted in Fine, Jon. "The Biz: Teen Title Crush Leads to Circ Cuts," *Advertising Age* (7 July 2003): 21.

2. Janson, "The Biz," 21; see also Andrea, Haman, "New Spin-offs Intensify Teen Girl Magazine Competition," *Kidscreen* (1 Jul. 2001): 41.

3. *CosmoGirl* was published by Hearst from 1999-2008. Conde Nast launched *Teen Vogue* in 2003. *Elle Girl* was published in the U.S. from 2001-2006 by Hachette Filipacchi. *Teen People* was published by Time Warner from 1998-2007.

4. Barbara Hudson, "Femininity and Adolescence," in *Gender and Generation*, eds., Angela McRobbie and Mica Nava (London: MacMillan, 1984), 31-53.

5. Peggy Orenstein, *Schoolgirls: Young Women, Self-Esteem, and the Confidence Gap* (New York: Anchor Books, 1994) and Pipher, Mary. *Reviving Ophelia: Saving the Selves of Adolescent Girls* (New York: Pantheon, 1994).

6. Emilie Zaslow, *Feminism Inc.: Coming of Age in Girl Power Media Culture* (New York: Palgrave Macmillan, 2009), 13.

7. See for example, the discussion of girl power in Ilana Nash, *American Sweethearts: Teenage Girls in Twentieth-Century Popular Culture* (Bloomington, IN: Indiana University Press, 2006).

8. Sarah Projansky, *Watching Rape: Film and Television in Postfeminist Culture* (New York: NYU Press, 2001), 67.

9. Jessica K. Taft, "Girl Power Politics: Pop-Culture Barriers and Organizational Resistance" in *All About the Girl,* ed. Anita Harris (New York: Routledge, 2004), 69-78.

10. Robert Goldman, *Reading Ads Socially* (New York: Routledge, 1992), 131.

11. Angela McRobbie, *Feminism and Youth Culture: From Jackie to Just Seventeen* (London: Macmillan, 1991) and Dawn H. Currie, *Girl Talk: Adolescent Magazines and Their Readers* (Toronto: University of Toronto Press, 1995), 42.

12. Susan Hopkins, *Girl Heroes: The New Force in Popular Culture* (Pluto Press: Australia, 2002), 102.

13. Naomi Wolf, *The Beauty Myth: How Images of Beauty are Used Against Women* (New York: Doubleday), 1992).

14. Advertisement in *CosmoGirl,* 2001.

15. Advertisement in *Teen People,* 2004.

16. Advertisement in *CosmoGirl*, 2001.

17. Advertisement in *CosmoGirl*, 2001.

18. Advertisement in *CosmoGirl*, 2001.

19. Susan Faludi, *Backlash: The Undeclared War on American Women* (New York: Crown), 1991.

20. Advertisement in *Seventeen*, 2003-2004.

21. Advertisement in *YM*, 2003-2004.

22. Advertisement in *Teen People*, 2004.

23. Advertisement in *Teen People*, 2004.

24. Laura Vanderkam,"Teen 'Zines Hawk Fake Girl Power," *USA Today* 20 Feb. 2003, 13A.

25. Vanderkam, "Teen 'Zines", 13A.

26. Rosalind Gill, "Culture and Subjectivity in Neoliberal and Postfeminist Times," *Subjectivity* 25 (2008): 443.

27. Marnina Gonick, "Between 'Girl Power' and 'Reviving Ophelia': Constituting the Neoliberal Girl Subject," *NWSA Journal*, vol. 18, no. 2 (June 2006): 1-23.

28. Anthony Giddens, *Modernity and Self: Identity. Self and Society in the Late Modern Age* (Cambridge: Polity Press, 1991), 75.

29. Advertisement in *Seventeen*, 2003-2004.

30. Advertisement in *Teen People*, 2004.

31. Advertisement in *CosmoGirl* in 2001.

32. Advertisement in *CosmoGirl* in 2001.

33. Advertisement in *CosmoGirl* in 2001.

34. Advertisement in *Seventeen*, 2003-2004.

35. Advertisement in *Teen People*, 2004.

36. Advertisement in *Seventeen*, 2003-2004.

37. Advertisement in *Seventeen*, 2003.

38. Projansky, *Watching Rape*, 74.

39. Advertisement in *YM*, 2003-2004.

40. Advertisement in *CosmoGirl*, 2001.

41. Gonick, "Between 'Girl Power,'" 1-23.

42. Marisa Meltzer, *Girl Power: The Nineties Revolution in Music* (New York: Faber & Faber), 2010.

43. Hopkins, *Girl Heroes*, 28.

Chapter Two
Children and Media in *Parents* Magazine
by Amy Richards Franzini

"I believe the children are our future. Teach them well and let them lead the way."[1] Teach them well and let them lead the way . . . what is a parent or caregiver to do when he or she has questions regarding what to teach children, or how to teach them? Who teaches the parents? Parents, like children, of course, learn from example. But in today's society, example has expanded from the traditional family, tribe and culture to include the mass media.

An old African proverb says, "It takes a village to raise a child." Today's village includes not only neighbors, school and church, but also magazines, books, television and the Internet. We are always learning from the media, whether we are actively seeking information or not. But when parents do actively seek advice from the media, what is the media teaching them? And what happens when the advice parents are seeking is about the media itself? This chapter will explore what one specific member of the "media village," *Parents* magazine, advises parents about children's use of mass media.

The growth of parenting advice and education has been influenced by changes in medicine, sociology, media and more. Julia Grant,[2] Peter N. Stearns,[3] and Ann Hulbert[4] have intensively chronicled the history of parental education and advice. All of these parenting advice histories recognize the importance of *Parents* magazine to parental advice and education.

Steven Schlossman documented the introduction of *Parents* magazine and the challenges that went along with bringing scientific, psychological and sociological research to the masses.[5] As Schlossman described, *Parents* magazine was founded in 1926 (originally called *Children, The Magazine for Parents*) by George J. Hecht through funding of the Laura Spelman Rockefeller Memorial Foundation (a chief benefactor of the parent education movement).

15

From its beginnings, *Parents* tried to balance expert advice and common sense. According to Schlossman, *Parents* sold 100,000 copies a month within a year of its origin and reached almost a million subscribers by 1946. Today, *Parents* has over 2.2 million subscribers and close to 40,000 single-copy sales per month.[6]

Parents is just one magazine and magazines are just one form of media. Parenting advice is also solicited and transmitted through books, television programs and the Internet. A search for "parenting advice books" on online retailer Amazon.com nets 9,653 results.[7] A wider Internet search on parenting advice garners over 57 million search results. A. Rae Simpson provides an in-depth analysis of the role all mass media play in parenting advice.[8] But looking specifically at *Parents* magazine can provide a consistent glimpse into what is important to American parents as well as trends in expert advice on childrearing. As Stearns notes, "Child-rearing literature does not…clearly predict child-rearing practice or even parental attitudes. At the same time, people who buy such publications—who provide the subscriber base for an outlet like *Parents* magazine—clearly feel they have some need, and they are likely to assimilate some of the material presented to them."[9]

Mass media, including *Parents* magazine, communicate parenting advice about myriad issues ranging from sleeping and eating to discipline and morality. One specific topic of advice found in many parenting advice media addresses the media itself, or more specifically children's use of mass media. Again, magazines are not the only place a parent will find advice regarding children's use of mass media. One of the most well known experts in parenting advice, Dr. Spock, dedicates an entire chapter to the media in the most recent edition of his "essential" parenting book.[10] Similarly, William and Martha Sears dedicate the last chapter of their book *The Successful Child* to how parents should monitor media and technology influences.[11] Since most parenting advice media provide some sort of opinion on children's use of mass media, it is both interesting and important to explore how such a staple in parenting advice—the magazine *Parents*—advises parents about the mass media over time. Is the message consistent or contradictory? Is expert advice consistent with editorial opinion and advertising practices? Children—and children's media are "big business" — a billion dollar industry.[12] Many experts, such as the American Academy of Pediatrics[13] and the American Psychological Association[14] recommend limited children's media exposure, but can a publication that is dependent on advertising dollars truly encourage parents to curb their children's media use?

To answer these questions and discover how *Parents* magazine posits advice on children's media use, a content analysis of two years of *Parents* magazine was performed. Twenty-four consecutive issues of *Parents* magazine, from January 2008 through December 2009 were analyzed. All mentions of the mass media (books, music, television, internet, movies, and video/computer games) were examined, from quick suggestions ("Check out this movie") to in-depth articles. Any advertisements for mass media products were considered as well.

Parents Position on Children's Use of Mass Media

In the January 2008 issue of *Parents*, editor in chief, Sally Lee writes, "Parents across the country worry about the same things that concern me. Everything from the impact of the media on kids and the cost of health care to environmental hazards, education and difficulties balancing work and family."[15] setting a consistent tone on the periodical's position regarding the mass media. They recognize its ubiquitous nature, but are concerned about its impact on children. However, after careful evaluation of twenty-four issues of the periodical it is evident that it is not really the mass media that is of concern, it is two specific forms of media—television and the Internet. In fact, *Parents* does not even mention two forms of mass media, radio or magazines. Movies are mentioned, but there is not much focus. There is much focus, however on a last form of media . . . which was actually one of the first . . . books. There is an obvious dichotomy in *Parents'* position on children's use of mass media: books are good but television and the Internet are (mostly) bad. In another Letter from the Editor, Sally Lee illustrates that dichotomy in her own words:

A book—black words printed on a white page—can seem so irrelevant and old-fashioned, especially when kids can escape into virtual-reality games or their favorite TV shows served up on demand. But books play a huge role in every child's life. They not only help kids learn to read and write and express themselves, but they can exercise a child's imagination in a way no movie or video game can. And research shows that creative kids are smart kids. So tonight turn off the TV, tuck your little one in bed, and savor an extra bedtime story.[16]

Parents' view on books will be discussed first, then the Internet, and finally television. Video and computer games will be included in the Internet discussion and movies and DVDs will be included in the television discussion. For all forms of media, analysis revealed that discussion of media was found in four different ways: short recommendations of a specific media product; shorter articles (one page or less with no author byline); as part of an article about another issue (i.e. sleeping or eating); or longer, more in-depth articles specific to media. Discussion, therefore, will follow the same pattern.

Book Recommendations

A monthly feature in all issues of *Parents* is called "Goody Bag." It comprises approximately ten pages of content of the magazine (from around page 20 through page 30). Every month there was at least one book recommended, but some of the movies recommended were also based on books (for examples, *The Tale of Despereaux* and *Hotel for Dogs*). Many of the book recommendations found in the "Goody Bag" revolved around some theme for the month, such as bugs, dinosaurs, the United States or a holiday.

Another regular feature found in *Parents* is a brief interview with a celebrity who is starring in an upcoming movie or television program. While the television show or movie is obviously mentioned, many questions asked of the celebrities tend to be about books. For example, in the February 2008 issue, in an interview with actress Mary Louise Parker[17] (star of the film *The Spiderwick Chronicles*) two of the five interview questions were about reading and books: "Which books do you like to read to your children?" and "So, reading is pretty important in your family?" Also, in the March 2009 issue, actress Reese Witherspoon mentioned that she reads to her kids every night, and even provided her kids' favorite authors.[18]

In numerous articles in *Parents* magazine, writers suggested using books to help teach children certain life lessons, from eating, sleeping and potty training to independence, values and culture. For example, in an April 2008 article on death and grief,[19] *Parents* suggested four books to introduce the topic to children: *When Dinosaurs Die*; *What's Heaven?*; *The Forever Dog*; and *Freddie the Leaf*. Most of the articles dealt with a moral and behavioral qualities parents are supposed to value in their children: patience, cooperation, honesty, perseverance, compassion, loyalty, teamwork, responsibility, generosity, self-worth, gratitude, respect and empathy. Other recommendations were designed to assist with some sort of activity a child might experience, such as getting surgery, moving to a new city or starting a new school.

One article actually combined the morality/behavioral issue with the love of reading, by suggesting using books to learn about other cultures. Seemingly, if parents follow this advice their children will not only love reading, but love other cultures as well. The article provides six book suggestions for babies, six for toddlers, and six for preschoolers, in which, as the title of the article suggests, they can read "Around the World One Story at a Time."[20]

Over a two-year period, there was one in-depth article about reading and books in *Parents*. The March 2008 issue featured a three-page article entitled, "Raise a Reader"[21] which included strategies to help parents instill a love of reading in their children. The article was organized by age, from baby, toddler, preschool, up through kindergarten and discussed what each age group learns from reading at these different stages, as well as suggestions for making reading fun at this stage. Also included are the five "best books ever" for each age group to help get parents started.

Internet and Video Game Recommendations

There were fewer suggestions for websites and videogames than there were for books and visual media (television, movies and film). A couple of websites relevant to Black History Month were included in the February 2008 issue. In May 2008 a brief article about "hot toys" included toys that have social websites associated with them.[22] The December 2008 issue featured "The Best Video Games Right Now"[23] for different age groups and by type (physical, creative, brainteasers, etc.) just in time for the holiday shopping season. While there was one short article that illustrated a positive aspect of video games (a blurb about TeachTown, a computer game designed for autistic children)[24], most articles about the internet and video games focused on the negative aspects of the medium and were written as cautionary tomes to parents: Beware of the Internet! Beware of Video Games! It is not surprising that in a January 2008 article that reported the results of a *Parents* poll, 50 percent of parents "are extremely worried about sexual predators on the internet—the same number that are worried about predators in our neighborhoods."[25] One enters into a chicken-or-egg debate with fear of sexual predators on the Internet: Are parents more afraid because the media focuses more coverage on the issue, or does the media focus more coverage on the issue because parents are afraid? According to a short paragraph in June 2009, the "Real Risk Kids Face Online"[26] is not sexual predators, but rather bullies. These shorter articles tended to quote one or two sentences from a research study, pull out one statistic that will cause alarm in parents and leave it at that. The one statistic for this short blurb was "42% of kids bullied on the Web are also harassed at school." These shorter articles focused more on fear than on solutions or suggestions.

In another example from August 2009, one statistic was given regarding video game addiction, "A new study . . . found that almost one in ten gamers ages 8 to 18 show signs of addiction."[27] In this case, however, *Parents* not only provided the alarming statistic (with no background of the study) but also four short suggestions for parents to follow to avoid their children becoming a statistic.

While there were no mentions of the Internet and video games in larger articles related to other topics, such as sleeping and eating, there were two feature-articles about online safety.

A February 2008[28] article discussed the risks present when children go online (such as being exposed to inappropriate content, overuse of the Internet and sharing of personal information). *Parents* then provided caretakers with a "rule book" for Internet safety. This follows the pattern seen above in sharing alarming, fearful information with parents and then providing them with tools to avoid their fear becoming a reality (this is similar to the advertising tactic of creating a consumer need and then having your product fulfill that need).

Again in September 2008,[29] the magazine included an article (even recycling the article name, "Safety 'Net") on protecting children online, again listing "rules" to follow, and also suggesting safe social sites for young children. There was little, if any, discussion of the positives of the Internet (access to information, connection to others), rather, the focus was negative and seemed designed to instill fear in parents: be wary of the Internet.

While the negatives of the Internet were a primary focus on media discussion in *Parents* magazine, the most negative discussion revolved around television.

Television, Film, and DVD Recommendations

There were few specific recommendations for children's television programs during the period studied. In September 2008,[30] *Parents* recommended four new programs as the best of the new fall season, *Imagination Movers* (Disney Channel), *Toot & Puddle* (National Geographic and Noggin), *Martha Speaks* (PBS), and *Sid the Science Guy* (PBS). Similarly, in September 2009[31], they recommended *Angelina Ballerina: The Next Step* (Nickelodeon). There were many DVD and movie recommendations, however, at least one per month. In the two-year period studied, there were at least twenty recommendations for in-theater movies, and at least twenty for home DVDs. For example, in February 2009[32], *Parents* recommended having a family movie night and suggested some DVDs to watch: *The Wizard of Oz, Mary Poppins, Annie, Little Mermaid*, and *Sleeping Beauty.*

Like the short articles that quoted research studies found related to the Internet, *Parents* offered similar coverage of research relating to television. In September 2009,[33] a brief quote from a research study was presented that simply said, "The more that kids are exposed to programming intended for adults, the more likely they are to become sexually active at an earlier age. "The quote referred to research performed by the Center on Media and Child Health at Children's Hospital Boston, but there were no details of the study provided for the readers, just that quote. By simply providing a finding, the magazine reader is left to assume the study proved that watching adult program caused kids to become sexually active at an early age. There was no background to how the study was performed, no explanation to the idea of correlation. A relationship between the two variables that may have some causal influence, but that influence could in fact be the other way around: kids who were sexually active at an earlier age were also attracted to adult programming. Of course it is more likely that there a number of factors that caused both of those statistics, including social status and educational background, to name just two. But readers are never given that full picture unless they choose to seek out the original study and read for themselves. *Parents,* and all popular periodicals for that matter, just quote the scary statistic. This begs the question, do readers then think that if they stop that one behavior their children will not have sex at an early age? Another short blurb in the February 2008 issue cautions:

> Boys who watch violent TV shows or movies (like Star Wars, SpiderMan and Power Rangers) between ages 2 and 5 are more likely to be antisocial or aggressive at ages 7 to 10, according to a new study in Pediatrics. Surprisingly, violent programming had no effect on girls' behavior patterns, possibly because the "violent" shows that girls chose to watch had more hostile language and threatening behavior than physical violence."[34]

Again, there was no mention of the specifics of the study. Readers were not informed on how this violent behavior was observed by the researchers: did they hit, was it in a natural or laboratory setting, or was it based on the reporting from parents. Again, parents are not given enough information to decide if this correlation between television programming and behavior was just that—a co-relationship—or if there was truly causation, and that it was the programming causing the aggression and not the other way around. By boiling down an entire research project to one quotation, the magazine is telling parents that if you limit your boys' watching of these types of programs then your boys will not be aggressive; while hopeful, this is unrealistic.

While these two examples highlight the negative tilt that *Parents* has towards television and video, it is important to note that they did provide one positive example of the use of video for children. The November 2008[35] issue describes a Sesame Workshop video, entitled *Here for You*, that can be used to help kids deal with serious illness and being in the hospital (that is available to view directly from their website).[36]

A December 2009[37] article about race relations mentions how television or movies can be used to talk to your children about race. This one positive use of the television was drowned by numerous instances of blaming television for some sort of problem when part of larger discussions on other issues. For instance, an article on eating cites television as one reason why children might have eating issues.[38] In an article about talking to children about sex, television was mentioned as one reason why such a talk may be warranted.[39] Concern about a child's irritating behavior? Perhaps she's copying it from television.[40] Does a parent's son lack focus in school? Beware of television![41] While these examples explicitly blame the media, still others implicitly lay blame on the media through recommendations regarding other behaviors: no television while you eat, don't let your kids watch television during a playdate, no television before bedtime, and so on.

One of the focused articles on television follows the pattern noted in the shorter article section previously discussed, by depending on statistics and fear. A July 2008 article,[42] written in question and answer format combines almost every fear a parent might have about television (and all the fears that are highlighted by popular rhetoric): obesity, smoking, sexual risks, eating disorders, substance abuse, violence and fear. Parent-readers who lets their children watch television after reading this would most certainly be harboring some guilt. The same issues discussed in the previous paragraphs about dependence on statistics and correlative studies relate here, but there was one other relevant finding relating to this article. One question in the article asked, "Is educational programming better?" The expert answered, "There are no positive effects for children under age 2. Their brains are not yet developed enough to learn from a screen. Even the 'baby videos' might contribute to cognitive delays and cause real harm."[43] Still, in the twenty-four issues of *Parents* from 2008 through 2009, there were actually nineteen advertisements for such baby-learning videos (eight for a DVD program called *Preschool Prep*, two for *Baby Einstein*, two for *Muzzy* language system, one for *Sparkabilities*, and one for *Your Baby Can Read*).

When asked if there were any positive effects of television, the expert replied, "For children older than 2, some educational programs can improve language skills….and age-appropriate nonviolent video games can help kids learn about problem solving."[44] But according to this article, there are no positives aspects to children watching "entertainment" programming. This negative, expert view was complemented by a more down-to-earth, realistic approach from a non-expert, parent-author, in a June 2009 article that offers a glimpse into the positive possibilities of television.[45] It discussed parents' involvement in their children's viewing and teaching kids to become critical viewers. This author accepted that while not for everyone, television is typically a part of family life. The author offered a more commonsense approach: parents shouldn't allow their children to watch anything and everything; they should teach selective viewing. While the author did mention the American Academy of Pediatrics screen time suggestion of no more than two hours a day, she asked the parents to make those decisions thoughtfully for their own children. She mentioned, "Used properly, the small screen can provide great fodder for everything from critical-thinking skills to talking to your kid about values—yours and his . . . The challenge is to make tube time an active experience by watching television with your child and by encouraging him to think carefully and develop opinions about what he sees."[46] Further, the author provided online resources for parents to help make common sense television viewing with their children a reality.

Advertising

While much of the editorial content regarding television (and movies/DVDs) was negative, *Parents* still featured advertising for mass media products. A previous section mentioned the advertising for baby-learning DVDs, and there were also many advertisements for entertainment DVDs (thirty-five), but just three for actual television programs (although many of the DVDs were related to television programs). This is not surprising given that magazines depend not only on subscribers but also on advertising. Still, parent-readers may be confused when they read about the fact that screen time is inappropriate for their fifteen-month old, and then see advertisements for a bevy of products suggesting that letting her watch *Preschool Prep* or *Baby Einstein*, will actually make her smarter and not damage her for life. The emergence of all of these products designed to make babies smarter is deserving of investigation.

Conclusion

As discussed in the previous sections, analysis of twenty-four issues of *Parents* magazine revealed that the magazine holds a positive editorial position involving books, but is cautious and distrustful of the Internet (and video games) and television (and movies). While some articles provided parents with constructive uses for the Internet and television, for the most part, they were seen as something to be feared—something that can hurt children. But why? In her book *It's Not the Media: The Truth about Pop Culture's Influence on Children*[47], Karen Sternheimer argues that it is precisely because it is easier to blame a nameless, faceless enemy than to look at the "real" problems in society, like poverty, public schools and support for families, and how easy it is for popular culture to be the scapegoat. Sternheimer reminds us that fear sells, and by coupling fear with children, we strike a chord that will continue to get attention, and mask that real problems at bay. As she states, "Fear can be crippling, especially when we fear something that poses no major threat. While changing media culture may truly concern us at times, we need to be sure to keep our real challenges in sight."[48]

The way that *Parents* incorporates books into most of their editorial content provides hope as to how all mass media can be used to help. Just as *Parents* offers suggestions of books to help with bullying or grief, perhaps they could suggest a movie like *Karate Kid* or *My Girl*, where those same issues are portrayed. Rather than focusing only on the negative, if a magazine like *Parents* suggested ways to use the entertainment programs that children are watching to help them with physical, cognitive, social, psychological and cultural issues they are dealing with, the world might not be such a scary place after all.

Notes

1. Linda Creed (lyricist), "The Greatest Love of All." Alfred Publishing, 1977.
2. Julia Grant, *Raising Baby by the Book* (New Haven: Yale University Press, 1998).
3. Peter N. Stearns, *Anxious Parents: A History of Modern Childrearing in America* (New York: New York University Press, 2003).
4. Ann Hulbert, *Raising America: Experts, Parents, and a Century of Advice About Children* (New York: Vintage Books, 2003).
5. Steven Schlossman, "Perils of Popularization: The Founding of Parents Magazine." In *History and Research in Child Development: In Celebration of the Fiftieth Anniversary of the Society*, ed. Alice Boardman Smuts and John W. Hagan. (Chicago: University of Chicago Press, 1986), 65–77.
6. Audit Bureau of Circulations. Verified and Analyzed Non-Paid Magazine Publisher's Statement for Parents Magazine for the six months ended June 30, 2009.
7. Amazon.com, www.amazon.com (accessed April 29, 2012).
8. A. Simpson, *The Role of Mass Media in Parenting Education* (Boston: Center for Health Communication, Harvard School of Public Health, 1997).

9. Peter N. Stearns, *Anxious Parents: A History of Modern Childrearing in America* (New York: New York University Press, 2003), 19.

10. Benjamin Spock, M.D. and Robert Needlman, M.D. *Dr. Spock's Baby and Child Care* (8th edition) (New York: Pocket Books, 2004).

11. William Sears, M.D. and Martha Sears, R.N., *The Successful Child: What Parents Can Do to Help Kids Turn Out Well* (New York: Little, Brown, and Company, 2002).

12. James U. McNeal, *Kids as Customers: A Handbook of Marketing to Children* (New York: Lexington Books, 1992), 232.

13. American Academy of Pediatrics, *Media Matters: A National Media Education Campaign* (2008), www.aap.org/advocacy/mmcamp.htm (accessed April 29, 2012).

14. American Psychological Association, *Policy Statement: Violence in Mass Media*, www.apa.org/about/governance/council/policy/media.aspx (accessed April 29, 2012).

15. Sally Lee, "Letter from the Editor," *Parents,* January 2008, 14.

16. Lee, "Letter," *Parents,* 10.

17. Anon., "Celeb Q&A," *Parents,* February 2008, 30.

18. Anon., "Goody Bag," *Parents,* March 2009, 24.

19. Christina Frank, "Saying Goodbye," *Parents,* April 2008, 64.

20. Barrie Gillies, "Around the World One Story at a Time," *Parents,* May 2009, 40–43.

21. Kim Ratcliff, "Raise a Reader," *Parents,* March 2008, 118-121.

22. Anon., "Toy Trends," *Parents,* May 2008, 28.

23. Warren Buckleitner, Ph.D. and Andrew Barnett, "The Best Video Games Right Now," *Parents,* December 2008, 184-188.

24. Anon. "Computer Games for Autistic Kids," *Parents,* June 2008, 40.

25. Anon. "What Keeps Parents Up at Night," *Parents,* January 2008, 20.

26. Anon. "The Real Risk Kids Face Online," *Parents,* June 2009, 34.

27. Anon. "Game Time," *Parents,* August 2009, 31.

28. Amanda Wolfe, "Safety 'Net," *Parents,* February 2008, 152–153.

29. Rebecca Felsenthal, "Safety 'Net," *Parents,* September 2008, 116–121.

30. Anon., "Best in Show," *Parents,* September 2008, 26.

31. Anon., "Tutu Thumbs Up," *Parents,* September 2008, 26.

32. Anon., "Pass the Popcorn!" *Parents,* February 2009, 141.

33. Anon., "Remote Control," *Parents,* September 2009, 38.

34. Anon., "Boys and TV," *Parents,* February 2008, 36.

35. Anon., "Make Hospitals Less Scary," *Parents,* November 2008, 42.

36. Sesame Workshop, "Our Work," www.sesameworkshop.org/initiatives/emotion/hereforyou (accessed April 29, 2012).

37. Katherine Whittemore, "Imagine a World," *Parents,* December 2009, 131.

38. Nancy Gottesman, "Mealtime Crimes," *Parents,* March 2008, 152.

39. Jeannette Moninger, "No-Dread Sex Ed," *Parents,* April 2009, 181.

40. Jeannette Moninger, "Enough of That," *Parents,* September 2009, 234.

41. Anon. *Parents,* "Boys Will Be Boys," April 2008, 54-58.

42. Janna Oberdorf, "Too Much Television," *Parents,* July 2008, 40-43.

43. Oberdorf, "Television?," *Parents,* 40–43.

44. Oberdorf, "Television?," *Parents,* 40–43.

45. Judy Goldberg, "Be Your Kid's TV Guide," *Parents,* June 2009, 178–182.

46. Goldberg, "Be Your Kid's," Parents, 178–182.

47. Karen Sternheimer, *It's Not the Media: The Truth about Pop Culture's Influence on Children* (Boulder, CO: Westview Press, 2003).
48. Sternheimer, *It's Not the Media*, 220.

Chapter Three
Making Kids Sexy: Sexualized Youth, Adult Anxieties, and Abercrombie & Fitch
by Stephen Gennaro

Introduction

Even the least critical consumers of media images must admit that there is something different to how Abercrombie & Fitch does business. While many companies over the last century have used sex and innuendo to enhance the desirability of their products and increase sales, Abercrombie & Fitch at times appears to be selling the sexualization of youth itself, with its clothing lines as the simple run-off or side effect of consuming the lifestyle associated with their products. Whether it is in their magalogues, at their clothing stores, or on their company website, the connection between Abercrombie & Fitch and sexualized youth is difficult to ignore. Abercrombie & Fitch is not a small company, producing images and representations of youth and sexuality in isolation. The company itself is over 115 years old, and in the 2007 fiscal year, Abercrombie & Fitch posted $3.8 billion in net sales. Therefore it falls under the same economic principles and factors that affect other major corporations in the marketplace. Its actions and goals are always influenced by its priority, which is to make money. However, because of its sheer size and its saturation in the marketplace, its advertisements also maintain a social role (and not necessarily by choice). Because Abercrombie & Fitch is a business, it is under no obligation to respect the social role that it plays and therefore create unbiased advertisements. And since ads don't happen by accident, consumers cannot lose sight of the fact that advertisements are ideological texts. Ideological texts always come with a bias and an unequal power dynamic. Remembering that ideology works on both explicit and implicit levels, images and representations of youth at Abercrombie & Fitch have tended to focus at the explicit level on a romanticized, sexualized, and innocent youthfulness. This nostalgic representation of youth presents youth not as a biological stage in life, but as a lifestyle and a feeling, no different from happiness or wealth, and something to which everyone should aspire. However, implicitly, representations of youth in advertisements have tended to draw on the deeper psychological motivations of adolescence that, it was suggested by discourses in adolescent psychology in the early twentieth century are to be experienced by everyone, namely the competing sexual identities and desire for approval from the peer group.[1]

A quick visit to the Abercrombie & Fitch website can reveal a significant amount about the company's focus in marketing and in the reasoning behind the media publicity over the last decade surrounding Abercrombie & Fitch's sexualization of youth. When visitors to the Abercrombie & Fitch website view the images under the category of "men's" or 'women's" and clicks on the subheading of *A&F Book* they are immediately introduced to representations of adults in youthful scenarios, engaging in youthful activities, and in all cases framed with an overly-sexualized youthful exuberance. Even the models themselves are staged to appear adolescent and prepubescent; note the extremely petite body frames and the complete absence of body, facial, and pubic hair, even though the lower midriffs of the models are exposed. Here the ideas of youth are closely connected to a romanticized and nostalgic representation of youth as witnessed through the positive feeling associated with a highly sexualized identity. However, absent from these over-sexualized images of an innocent youthful sexuality is the struggle and tension characteristic of the Sturm und Drang of adolescence and the competing sexual selves that psychologists such as Hall and Freud posited were universal to the experiences of youth.[2]

At the same time as the images of adults in the "men's" and "women's" sections of the Abercrombie & Fitch website are framed and sold to the consuming public as sexualized youth, the images in the gallery on the Abercrombie & Fitch website under the category of "kids" (www.abercombiekids.com) are famed in exactly the same fashion as the adult advertisements. This is reminiscent of the marketing discourse of perpetual adolescence, which suggests that the representation of "youth" (as both a category of distinction and as a lifestyle commodity itself for consumption) have created a marketplace where the traditional markers of delineation between adolescence and adulthood have been erased (Gennaro, "Purchasing" 120). The term, *perpetual adolescence*, describes the ways that the contemporary American culture industry trains both young and old to be consumers of "youth" in a marketplace that privileges adolescence over adulthood. By doing so, American society has effectively erased the traditional lines of distinction between adulthood and adolescence. The result of this blurring of lines and boundaries is the removal of youth as a category connected to biological growth and is instead replaced with youth as a feeling or lifestyle available to all for purchase.

Given the current media attention surrounding the sexualization of youth (both in the presentation of children as sexualized beings and in the representation of youthfulness as a desirable commodity and focus of gaze), this chapter will address perpetual adolescence in the context of youthful sexuality, and especially how it speaks to contemporary anxieties about the issue. The questions this chapter seeks to explore are: where, if at all, does sexuality figure in this discourse, and furthermore, does the notion of perpetual adolescence defuse or exacerbate the contemporary panic about the marketing of sexualized sexuality? To address current anxieties about sexualized youth in advertising it is important to examine the discourses surrounding youth and how these discourses, which have a longer history than first glance would suggest, play such a critical role in the current representations of youth and the fears, hopes, dreams, and concerns of adults that these representations so profoundly inoculate.

A case study of Abercrombie & Fitch's highly controversial catalogue, which was taken out of print by the company in 2003 but returned to after a five year hiatus, is looked at to further explore the connection between sexualized youth and adult anxieties in contemporary North American society. It is important to note that this chapter is not analyzing the representations of sexualized youth in Abercrombie & Fitch advertisements in order to place judgment on the morality, social consciousness, or artistic and aesthetic value of the works. This chapter is not interested in the debate of whether or not Abercrombie & Fitch should be making these ads and displaying them in public places where young people have access to them. Instead, this paper is interested in how representations which frame youth as overly sexualized, care-free, nostalgic, and at the same time innocent, fall in line with over three centuries of representation, and continue to speak more to the fears, anxieties, hopes, ambitions, and ideals of adults in society than to the children they claim to represent. Therefore, inside the discussion of Abercrombie & Fitch's representation of youth in both adult and kids advertisements found in the 2008 magalogue, in stores, and on the company website are two sides to the current debate surrounding the sexualization of youth and its connection to perpetual adolescence: namely, the continuation of the Romantic and Puritan discourses of childhood, and what Lawrence Grossberg termed the peda-philic (child-loving) and peda-phobic (child-hating) representations of children in the media (4).

Two of the current discourses about children—the Romantic, and Puritan— can be traced back almost 400 years in Western culture. A closer look at the Romantic and Puritan, discourses about childhood reveal a significant amount of information about the power relations between children and adults, and the social role(s) of children at any given point in modern western history. The social construction of childhood found in both the Romantic and Puritan discourses about children have influenced the current construction of "childhood" as a category of distinction, and can best describe the anxieties around the sexualization of children that are so prevalent at the current moment. They position children as different from adults and often represent children as adults in training or as innocent, naïve youngsters in need of protection.

Both the Romantic and Puritan discourse about childhood tend to be viewed in discussion with John Locke's ideas of children as blank slates. John Locke, in his chapter "Of Ideas in General" posited the notion that we are all born tabula rasa, as a blank slate, and learn through our sensory perception of and experiences in our surrounding environment. Building on the idea of tabula rasa in his 1692 piece "Some Thoughts Concerning Education," Locke wrote that children were a blank slate upon which a society instructs, informs, and educates young people to meet the expectations and desires of that particular society. Locke's advice for educating children was simple: "[w]e must look upon our children, when grown up, to be like ourselves, with the same passions, the same desires" (3:41). As such, Locke argued for "parents and governors always to carry this in their minds that children are to be treated as rational creatures" (3:54). Although Locke did fundamentally believe that children were rational beings and should be treated in similar fashion to adults in terms of education and discipline, his argument outlined how the focus of education should be to model the appropriate behaviour for children so as to mold them into the types of healthy functioning citizens based on the desires of the adult.

What makes Locke's ideas problematic is his linking of the notion of the blank slate and the child to innate childhood innocence. For instance, when discussing why an adult should not lie to a child, Locke wrote, "We are not to entrench upon truth in any conversation, but least of all with children; since if we play false with them, we not only deceive their expectation, and hinder their knowledge, but corrupt their innocence, and teach them the worst of vices" (4:120). This notion of childhood innocence is problematic because it presupposes that adults know what is best for children and that therefore it is in the best interest of the children to have the expectations of their behaviour dictated to them. The notion of innocence—and its potential loss and corruption by adults—would lay at the heart of the Romantic Movement, where artists such as Rousseau would construct a romanticized notion of childhood that remains central to our understanding of children today.

The Romantic Discourse of Childhood

The Romantic discourse is most closely tied to Rousseau and his work *Emile*, where he speculated that the best way to educate a male child, like Emile, was to remove the child from social pressures and allow him to be free from guidance and discipline in the first several years of his life. The individual, according to Rousseau, would learn best from an opportunity to experience nature for himselves without regimented and forced expectations: "The help that one gives them should be limited to what is real utility, without granting anything to whim or to desire without reason; for whim will not torment them as long as it has not been aroused, since it is no part of nature" (1:172). Rousseau's ideas were further emphasized by others in the Romantic movement, in poems like William Wordsworth's "Ode" and William Blake's "Songs of Innocence and Songs of Experience," which suggested that childhood was a more pure time where the individual was uncorrupted by the evils of an industrialized society. The Romantics viewed the child as closer to nature and closer to God, and viewed childhood nostalgically as a greater time in one's life. There are several dangers inherent in this type of discourse, most notably the nostalgic ideals that are attached to youth, and the essentializing of childhood, which then suggests that a positive childhood is a time that is universal to all. By suggesting that everyone experiences childhood in the same fashion, the nostalgic ideals of childhood that are linked to the construct of a universal child hide the unequal power relations between and adult and child at the same time as they create an artificial and therapeutic felling around the happiness experienced in childhood. Today, such Romantic discourse is seen in the focus on youth and youthful sensibilities by companies such as Abercrombie & Fitch seeking to connect adult consumers with a happiness that is nostalgically associated with universal childhood experiences (www.abercrombie.com). For example, in each of the adult advertisements taken from the Abercrombie & Fitch website, the adult models are framed in youthful scenarios (i.e. holding a football), against a pastoral or Romantic back drop, and with accompanying text that "de-ages" the advertisement's readers and potential customers by suggesting, for example, that "young love is a flame" and is "fierce" much like those who purchase and wear Abercrombie & Fitch fashions (www.abercrombie.ca).

The construct of the universal child refers to the institutionalization of childhood, so that childhood can be seen a distinct category in the lives of all people, in which all people have similar experiences. As Harry Hendrick points out in his essay "Constructions and Reconstructions of British Childhood: An Interpretative Survey, 1880 to the Present":

> In 1800 the meaning of childhood was ambiguous and not universally in demand. By 1914, the uncertainty had been resolved and the identity determined, at least to the satisfaction of the middle class and respectable middle class. A recognizable "modern" notion was in place: childhood was legally, legislatively, socially, medically, psychologically, educationally, and politically institutionalized. (7)

During the nineteenth century the ideology of the universal child became crystallized in Western culture, so that by 1914 a definitive portrait of the innocent, naïve, and playful child in need of protection had become the dominant representation of what it meant to be young. This is important to my discussion, since it is the images of the universal child that the culture industries would use to first segment the marketplace and later fragment the segmented markets in an attempt to sell "youth" itself as a commodity. The construct of the universal child in an American context is what Nicholas Sammond in *Babes in Tomorrowland* calls "the generic American child," one that was "white (largely male), Protestant, and middle-class" (2). This generic American child surfaced in the twentieth century through the emerging social scientific and psychological discourses about adolescence, in addition to the rise of mass consumerism and continual advancements in information and communication technologies. For both Hendrick and Sammond, the construction of a universal or generic child suggested that one representation of children's behavior, childhood expectations, and childhood experiences eventually came to not only signify, but define, what it meant to be a child in the West. For Abercrombie & Fitch, the images of "adult" and "child" in their advertisements define their ideal customer by suggesting that it the universal child that personifies the "youth" Abercrombie & Fitch inherently sells with its products.

Of course, one of the largest problems with the construct of the universal child is who is left voiceless or absent from representation within such a totalizing discourse and how are issues such as gender, sexuality, race, or class obfuscated by a discourse that privileges white, male, and middle-class as normal. Furthermore, for companies such as Abercrombie & Fitch that are selling a notion of youth that is framed through this construct; how do they deal with these absences? This is not a new critique of Abercrombie & Fitch, who "in 2004 . . . agreed to pay $50 million to settle a lawsuit that accused the company of promoting whites over minorities and cultivating a virtually all-white image"(MSNBC.com). And while the company was able to quiet the critique of its privileging of a universal construct of youth in its advertisements, little has changed since 2004 (www.abercrombie.com). For example, in examining the advertisements of Abercrombie & Fitch found on their website, all the ads to be viewed portray only white, middle-class models, while at the same time portraying a distinctly Romantic and nostalgic sense of youthfulness (i.e. playing football, or rolling in the hay) that is framed as being experienced by all.

The Puritan Discourse of Childhood

Opposing the Romantic discourse of childhood, the Puritan discourse was largely a construction of an eighteenth century moral panic about children, although it was tied to the evangelical movements of the Puritans in the sixteenth to seventeenth century in both England and the United States. According to the Puritan discourse, children are born inherently evil because of the Christian notion of original sin; therefore, the child needs to be punished for its sins. The child needs guidance and protection not only from itself, but also from evils and perils of society, to ensure that its soul can be saved. Children's literature at the time reflected this moral panic: writers such as Maria Edgeworth in works like "The Orangeman," or Hannah More in "Betty Brown," warned children (usually in fairly graphic fashion) about the dangers of acting in a socially unacceptable fashion through didactic stories, which stressed the religious values and Protestant work ethic of the surrounding society. The endings of stories like "Betty Brown" provide an example to the reader of how the child in the story learns through her error and subsequent punishment that the path to success and happiness can only come through a continual focus on hard work and increased focus on morality. Terminology commonly associated with the Puritan discourse portrays children as inherently evil, angry, violent, and dangerous; it therefore positions children as being in need of structure and guidance. The danger of the Puritan discourse is that it suggests that childhood has universal negative qualities to be found in all children at all times and places, although the discourse itself draws from a specific historical Christian doctrine. Furthermore, it suggests that the child is in need of an ideological construction of actions and behavior and should not be given any access to power or decision making of his or her own. Today, the Puritan discourse can be seen in the focus on the protection of the child and it is precisely this evangelical construction of the child that parent groups opposed to Abercrombie & Fitch advertisements continually return to in their protesting and boycotting of the company. Whereas the Romantic discourse was built upon a universal construct of the generic child, the Puritan discourse of childhood is built underpinned by the ideas of development and progress in adolescent psychology that suggests that there are key stages of a child's (physical, emotional, and mental) evolution common to all, which are associated with a successful childhood and the creation of a healthy adult who can be productive in society (Sprinthall & Collins 24). An understanding of the ideas of adolescent psychology are essential both to the discourse of perpetual adolescence and to more clearly understanding the current debate surrounding the sexualization of youth as best witnessed in the discussion of Abercrombie & Fitch advertisements.

The Creation of the "Adolescent" and Its Connection to the Market

There are a series of ideas surrounding the development of children that are the basis of study for the field of adolescent psychology and to which the field of psychology is in general agreement. Usually the discussion of adolescence revolves around (or can be grouped into) the development of adolescents in five main areas: physical, cognitive, emotional, social, and behavioral development (Sprinthall & Collins 28). And in much the same way that the image of the universal child or generic American child has become a stand-in for all children in media representations of youth, so too have the ideas expressed in adolescent psychology become a stand-in for what is considered the normal transpiring of all adolescents:

> Adolescence is, among other things, an organized set of expectations closely tied to the structure of adult society. It stands out from the other stages of human development as a period of preparation rather than fulfilment . . . But Adolescence is a phase of imminence that is not quite imminent enough, of emergent adult biology that is

not yet completely coordinated with adult roles, of hopes that are not yet seasoned by contact with adult reality and of peer culture and society that mimic those of adults but are without adult ambitions or responsibilities. Adolescents are in a state of preparing themselves for adulthood by experimenting, studying, resisting, or playing. (qtd. in Sprinthall & Collins 3)

Our current understanding of the term *adolescence* has emerged out of the field of psychology and its understanding that adolescence is a stage in natural human development. According to psychological discourses about children, adolescence is an "in-between" period that separates childhood from adulthood. In viewing adolescence as a separate period, its participants (adolescents) are seen as having a series of actions, feelings, and self-understandings different from those who have yet to enter this stage and those who have successfully completed it. Psychologists claim that adolescence is as a period of change, where the individual experiences changes physically, mentally, ideologically, emotionally, and sexually. Partly, this change is necessary both to enter into this stage, usually around the age of twelve (with the onset of puberty), and for the completion of this period (to which psychologists cannot agree on an age, but which is usually seen to be sometime in the late teens or early twenties) through the mastering of those changes. Following in this train of thought, adolescence is not an option; it is a stage that everyone must pass through, and is as natural as birth and death. However, each culture creates the restrictions and expectations for adolescence based on the anxieties, aspirations, and desires of its adult population. It is against these restrictions and expectations that youth are forced to endure the training period of destabilization that psychologists have termed "adolescence" where they become the focus and subject of the projection of these adult anxieties and desires. The marketing discourse of perpetual adolescence suggests that the processes of adolescence still begin in early puberty but no longer end at (and indeed, they extend into) adulthood. Therefore, childhood as a social construction and adolescence as a medical discourse is the starting point for the discussion about how the marketing discourse of perpetual adolescence entered into the advertising agency and came to be the dominant practice of representation in advertisements in the new millennium.

The internal structure of the Abercrombie company itself is set up much like the psychological discourses of adolescence that aim to breakdown and segment "growing up" into distinguishable, identifiable categories:

Valued at $5 billion [in 2006], the company now has revenues approaching $2 billion a year rolling in from more than 800 stores and four successful brands. For the kids there's Abercrombie, aimed at middle-schoolers who want to look like their cool older siblings. For high-schoolers there's Hollister, a wildly popular surf-inspired look for "energetic and outgoing guys and girls" that has quickly become the brand of choice for Midwestern teens who wish they lived in Laguna Beach, Calif. (Denizet-Lewis, Salon.com).

However, the stages of adolescent consumerism don't end with the teenage years for the Abercrombie Company.

When the Hollister kids head off to college, Jeffries (referring to Michael S. Jeffries, chairman and chief executive at Abercrombie & Fitch) has a brand—the preppy and collegiate Abercrombie & Fitch—waiting for them there. And for the post-college professional who is still young at heart, Jeffries recently launched Ruehl, a casual sportswear line that targets twenty-two to thirty-five year-olds (Denizet-Lewis, Salon.com).For companies like Abercrombie & Fitch, youthfulness is a marketing strategy employed for the selling of commodities. The company has neatly sectioned off its audience into smaller markets, and for each market there is a distinct strategy of advertising. However, common to all of the Abercrombie & Fitch stores and clothing lines is a regular framing of youth and youthfulness as an inherent by-product to all the items for sale. Therefore, tied into each symbol or representation of youth is an economic equation, thought out in advance, preplanned and packaged for consumption, which hides all the unequal power relations of capitalism inherent in the commercial production of childhood. In the same way that Charles Sarland argues that because children's literature is primarily written, published, and produced by adults for children (Sarland 1) it cannot be viewed as innocent or without ideological bias, advertisements for Abercrombie & Fitch are also texts and therefore are ideological; and ideology can never be separated from its economic base or power relations.

With regard to the representation of sexualized youth in the production of Abercrombie & Fitch advertisements, the rationale behind the production of the ads is similar to the ideas of niche and segmented marketing. For each product class, advertisers determine precisely the target clientele of that product class, and then pinpoint the psychological needs that are of the greatest importance to that specific target market and highlight them in the product's advertisements. The marketplace is segmented into thousands of smaller niche markets, with each product targeted to the desires of a specific niche. For example, in analyzing the market of customers over fifty-five, the mature market, George P. Moschis posits how the segmented mature market in America can actually be subdivided into four smaller niche markets, based on the dominant psychological needs of the consumer:

> The 53 million adults age 55 and over can be grouped into four segments [niche markets]: 1. healthy hermits, 2. ailing outgoers, 3. frail recluses, and 4. healthy indulgers. The results suggest that the model is more effective than some commonly used approaches not only in identifying prime segments for products and services, but also in suggesting viable marketing strategies for reaching specific segments of older consumers. (Moschis 17)

There is a difference between segmented markets and niche markets, as Shani and Chalasani explain:

"Market segmentation" is the process of breaking a large market into smaller and more manageable submarkets. The objective is to identify homogeneous submarkets which are significantly different from one another. The organization picks one or more of the identified segments and treats each as "a small mass market." Whereas "niche marketing" is the process of carving out a small part of the market, the needs of which are not fulfilled. By specializing along market, customer, product, or marketing mix lines, a company can match the unique needs. (Shani & Chalasani 58)

This is why the marketing discourse of perpetual adolescence is so prevalent in advertising. Companies like Abercrombie & Fitch use representations of sexualized youth for the selling of adult products in an attempt to reunite segmented markets by tapping into the discourses of adolescent psychology, like those that Hall and Freud deemed to be universal psychological struggles everybody experienced in their evolution from child to adult, thus creating one all-encompassing niche market. For Abercrombie & Fitch, both niche and segmented marketing are cornerstones to its marketing strategy that is *really* selling a lifestyle and not necessarily a clothing line. In a 1999 interview Abercrombie & Fitch chairman and chief executive Michael Jeffries explained "We're a life-style brand, projecting inside the store and outside the store the life style of a very specific target customer, the 18-to-22-year-old American college student." And in addressing how many customers are in fact older than this target age bracket, Jeffries responded that "college was a very wonderful time of life for most people" and that "we live in a society where everyone aspires to be young" (qtd. in Elliot, *New York Times*). Therefore, if this evolution (from child to adult) can be delayed, then the marketplace of consumers who share similar psychological needs can be extended and the product class that advertisers need to focus on in order to influence consumer behavior can be a significant portion of the marketplace rather than a smaller, segmented, niche market.

Perpetual Adolescence at Play? Abercrombie & Fitch's "Magalogue"

The marketing discourse of perpetual adolescence suggests that the processes of adolescence still begin in early puberty but no longer end at—indeed, they extend into—adulthood. The topic of a prolonged adolescence appears to have been an area of study for psychologists throughout the twentieth century. In 1923, in "A Typical Form of Male Puberty," Siegfried Bernfeld first introduced the term "prolonged adolescence" when examining European youth movements in the aftermath of the First World War. Bernfeld observed that "members of these groups presented a strong predilection for intellectualization and sexual representation, thus delaying the resolution of adolescent conflict and, in consequence, the personality consolidation of late adolescence" (qtd. in Blos 38). Fifty years later, psychoanalyst Peter Blos took up the topic of prolonged adolescence in his 1979 work *Adolescent Passage*. Blos examined prolonged adolescence in two eras: the years leading up to 1955, and from 1955 to 1977. Blos examined male adolescents in American, middle-class families who were between the ages of eighteen and twenty-two years old; he found that most of his subjects in both eras (although at higher levels during the second era) had delayed entrance into adulthood either through a longer attendance in school or through living at home and remaining financially dependent on their parents for a longer period of time. According to Blos, "Instead of the progressive push, which normally carries the adolescent into adulthood, prolonged adolescence arrests this forward motion with the result that the adolescent process is not abandoned but kept open-ended" (39). Blos's findings suggest that prolonged adolescence was dangerous because" [t]his dilemma leads to the contrivance of ingenious ways to combine childhood gratifications with adult prerogatives. The adolescent strives to bypass the finality of choices and options exacted at the close of adolescence" (39). The works of Bernfeld and Blos highlight one of the core arguments of this chapter: that discourses about what it means to be young and old are social constructions, that they are always in the process of being defined and redefined, and that media representations of youth over the last half-century have made the markers agreed upon in adolescent psychology as the end of adolescence and the beginning of adulthood no longer a standard against which we can judge who is young and who is old.

The content of Abercrombie & Fitch's customer magazine, *A & F Quarterly*, serves as an excellent example of adult anxieties about youthful sexuality and the representation of these anxieties through the marketing discourse of perpetual adolescence. The "Magalogue," the term associated with the *A & F Quarterly* after 1998 (since it was a combination of youth magazine and catalogue), "featured articles on a wide range of youth popular culture and lifestyle topics . . . Articles included advice, music and movie reviews, and profiles and interviews with celebrities" (Duke University Library). In fact, the 2008 re-issue of the magalogue contains almost 200 pages of photographs and articles without any product placement or advertisements for Abercrombie & Fitch clothing. This is a continuation of the format used in the 2002 magalogue where according to Dan Reines, the "approximate number of nude or partially nude models pictured in the first 119 pages of *A&F 2002* (including cover): 49" and the "number of those pages which do not appear to feature any Abercrombie & Fitch products at all . . . 12" (Reines, Nerve.com) The catalog was actually first published in 1909, but it was only after the company retooled its approach to consumers in 1992, by shifting away from the sporting goods, outdoorsman market to a focus on upscale youth that the contents inside the catalogue also shifted. In 1997 the first *A & F Quarterly* catalog was printed, and by 2003 when the publication was stopped, in large part due to consumer pressure, Abercrombie & Fitch was selling over 200,000 copies of each issue at a price of $6 per magalogue (Bhatnagar, CNN.com).

On 27 March, 2008, page six of the *New York Post* reported: "IT can't be pornography if it's art, right? Abercrombie & Fitch is releasing a new catalog by

Bruce Weber full of even sexier shots of scantily clad teen models—but this time, it will be sold only in London and priced at close to $200, like an art book" (Johnson, *New York Post*). The images of the magalogue were taken by photographer Bruce Weber, under the creative direction of Sam Shahid, both of whom had previously worked on advertising campaigns for clothing companies, including the controversial Calvin Klein campaign in the 1990s which also came under fire for an over sexualization of younger models (Bhatnagar, CNN.com). A 2008 report in the *International Herald Tribune* suggests that the 2008 magalogue operated with a budget of £150,000 (approximately 300,000 US) an issue (Britten). The return of the Abercrombie & Fitch magalogue with a price tag of close to $200, further illustrates how the marketing discourse of perpetual adolescence underlies advertising ideologies at Abercrombie & Fitch (since the price tag suggests an adult consumer, even though the images and representations inside the magalogue center on youth and youthfulness) and is directly tied to the social environment and adult anxieties surrounding sexuality and youth in 2008. The images of the 2008 magalogue were much like the images found in earlier versions of the *A&F Quarterly* (Reines) where adult models were positioned as heavily sexualized, while playing on a youthful, nostalgic, and Romantic representation of youth. For example, on the cover of the 2008 magalogue (www.trendhunter.com/trends/new-af-quarterly) the cover photo is of an adult model, staged to look young and innocent so as to position himself as both child and adult. The backdrop to the photo is pastoral and plays to a Romantic notion of the innocent child. Furthermore, the model himself is not clothed and although the photo shows only the top half of the model's body, there is the option for the viewer to believe that the model is wearing no clothes at all. In addition to the advertisements, the advice/style columns of the magalogue work to destabilize youth by suggesting that completion of adolescence, the acceptance of peers, and the self-acceptance of a coherent sense of self are all still works in progress. The discussion surrounding the Abercrombie & Fitch catalogue that led to the discontinuation of *A & F Quarterly* in 2003, by parent groups, religious organizations, and media watch-dogs, and that have recently resurfaced in public discourse since the return of the catalogue in spring 2008, have tended to paint a much less positive representation of youth. Here, under the umbrella of a moral panic and the demise of family values in current culture, youth is portrayed as vulnerable, innocent, and in need of protection. The discussion surrounding the magalogue in 2003 prior to its pulling speaks a great deal to the Puritan discourse of childhood, and the fears of adults surrounding the oversexualization of youth. Many of these concerns still exist and continue to be voiced against current advertisement used by Abercrombie & Fitch on their website (www.abercrombie.com) that tend to suggest through images and copy that being young, being sexual, and wearing Abercrombie & Fitch products are all intertwined. The Puritan discourse of childhood and its need for the protection of children because of their innocence is heavily connected to John Locke's idea of the blank slate and the discourse of the blank slate can often be linked to parents groups interested in censorship. Here the argument of parent groups suggests that children viewing images of people in sexually suggestive scenes will desire to remake those advertisements in their own lives and participate in similar sexual activities. The logic of this type of argument suggests that young people are blank slates on which social images, discourses, and representations write and create the behaviors of people. Therefore, since the child is innocent and easily manipulated, it is the duty of parents and community groups to protect the child from engaging with the evils of the surrounding society. This is precisely the type of argument that was cited in the boycott against Abercrombie & Fitch in 2003 because of the nudity and sexually suggestive images found in *A&F Quarterly*. For example, Kevin McCullough argues:

> In a day in which more parents than ever are concerned about the likelihood of their daughter getting pregnant, their child being sexually active long before they are mature enough to handle the consequences or the rampant spread of sexually transmitted diseases in the "younger than 20" demographic today—it's time to stop Abercrombie & Fitch. (McCullough, worldnetdaily.com)

McCullough claimed that the 2003 Christmas edition of *A&F Quarterly* contained over 45 sexually explicit images in the first 120 pages, before any advertisements for clothing even appeared. The dangers according to McCullough and parent groups who had been protesting against the over sexualization of youth in Abercrombie & Fitch ads since 1999, was that magazine/catalogues like *A&F Quarterly*, although targeted at a more "mature" audience, contain clothing and products for their kid lines, suggesting a younger readership. Since writers like McCullough and concerned parent groups viewed the child as a blank slate that was both innocent and desexualized, the openly sexualized depiction of youth appeared problematic to them and spoke directly to the fears and anxieties of parenting.

In response to the public backlash against his company, CEO, Michael Jeffries, took a stance much closer to the discourse associated with a Romantic notion of childhood. Jean Jacques Rousseau's ideas of the Romantic child *Emile* have been tied to terms such as "innocent," "pure," and "naïve." In Book 2 of *Emile*, Rousseau writes:

> [l]ove childhood, promote its pleasures, its lovable instincts. Who among you has not sometimes missed that age when laughter was always on our lips, and when the soul was always at peace? Why take away from these innocent little people the joys of a time that will escape them so quickly and gifts that could never cause any harm? Why fill with bitterness the fleeting days of early childhood, days which will no more return for them than for you? (213)

In a 2006 interview, when responding to the criticisms associated with the magalogue Jeffries was quick to rebut "That's just so wrong! I think that what we represent sexually is healthy. It's playful. It's not dark. It's not degrading!

And it's not gay, and it's not straight, and it's not black, and it's not white. It's not about any labels. That would be cynical, and we're not cynical! It's all depicting this wonderful camaraderie, friendship, and playfulness that exist in this generation and, candidly, does not exist in the older generation" (Denizet-Lewis, Salon.com). For Jeffries, the purchasing of Abercrombie & Fitch is not about the products as much as is it about the lifestyle associated with the products. His defense of Abercrombie & Fitch ads is about protecting the niche and segmented marketing practices of the company and the brand image that the letters *A&F* have come to symbolize.

Herein lies the contradiction between the two adult discourses about youth and how adult notions of youthful sexuality positions each of these discourses in society. On the one hand, adults view youth as sexually "at risk" and objectified, falling in line with the Puritan discourse of childhood and at the core of the peda-phobic protesting of sexualized youth in advertisements. On the other hand, adults view youth as sexually "at play" and eroticize the youthfulness of a more carefree time in their lives, falling in line with the Romantic discourse of childhood and the peda-philic desires that underpin the nostalgic representations of youth in ads. However, neither of these adult views of youth is in fact truly representative of children and instead speak much more to the anxieties, fears, hopes, and desires of adults. In his discussion of America as peda-philic (child-loving) and peda-phobic (child-hating), Lawrence Grossberg used youth as a way to examine a larger social phenomenon, namely, differing conceptions of modernity in American history and society and therefore one possible explanation for the divide between the American political right and the American political left (109–196). For Grossberg, kids have been the arena of political discourse over the last quarter century, and it is through discourse about children that all other political debates have been waged (8). Unfortunately for children, the debate surrounding children, in fact has very little to do with children themselves, and instead discussion about the future of America has been channeled through the discussion about how Americans should raise their children. This gives rise to the competing myths of childhood, where one side sees the child as innocent and the source of all that is good in America; the child is something that needs protection from society. The other side sees children as the source of crime and all that is wrong with society; children become something that society needs protection from. However, as the debate surrounding Abercrombie & Fitch has illustrated, it is not only the myths that we privilege in the representations of youth in our society, but also the cultural backlash or response to these representations that illustrates the peda-philic and/or peda-phobic tendencies of a society.

When Grossberg's ideas on the war on childhood are connected to the marketing discourse of perpetual adolescence and advertisements of sexualized youth at Abercrombie & Fitch, two things become visible about the cultural production of youth. First, the power brokers of the economy, most notable the culture industries and not those in politics are the driving cultural force in American society and therefore any change in the concept of childhood will ultimately start and end with media representations. Second, in acknowledging that the marketing discourse of perpetual adolescence in advertising is in fact a strategy of distinction, which seeks to use artificial desire as a way of convincing adults that they need to be youthful, a more simple answer appears as to why there are conflicting peda-philic (child as sexually at play) representations of youth and peda-phobic (child as sexually at risk) discourse in ensuing debate. After all, it is through the discourses of childhood, best represented in media that America continually redefines what it means to be a child, an adult, an individual, and a member of a family, a community, and a society.

Conclusion

Childhood is a social construction; however, discourse and representations of youth have real consequences in society. Adolescence is a category of discrimination in that a person's age and life positioning immediately reveal a whole category of subjective beliefs or stereotypes in the same way that a person's gender immediately implies a whole set of power relations. And although childhood is different from other social variables because it is a temporary space, the extension of this temporal space to a lifelong process is precisely the objective of the culture industries in the marketing discourse of perpetual adolescence.[3] Therefore, adolescence and childhood become socially constructed categories of distinction where relationships of power, domination, and inequality are continually contested. As Henry Jenkins suggests, "[T]his marginalization affects not only how we understand the child, its social agency, its cultural contexts, and its relations to powerful institutions, but also how we understand adult politics, adult culture, and adult society, which often circle around the specter of the innocent child" (Jenkins 6). If this is true, the larger question is why. Why expand childhood? Why delay adulthood? What are the benefits to a society for doing so? The sizeable grasp of economics and capitalism in Western societies plays a significant role in answering this question. By connecting the scientific and medical discourses of adolescent psychology to the advertising agency, we see that the "destabilization" of adolescence is a powerful marketing tool that allows for the selling of consumer goods and lifestyles, and that it is in the best interests of advertisers and the culture industries to keep the stress, duress, and anxieties of adolescence alive in all people, because this is what helps to trigger their desire to purchase consumer goods. The idea of segmenting children's lives into distinct categories, periods, or compartments to be analyzed and studied is in fact a marketing discourse that has become naturalized and invisible through its continual valorization in the media and in the medical and academic disciplines of adolescent, behavioral, and social psychology.[4] Explicitly, youth is represented as Romantic, innocent, pure, nostalgic, and something to be desired by all. Youth is represented as not only safer, stronger, more alive, and freer, but also as more powerful. Youth is no longer something directly tied to the biology of age. Implicitly tied into these representations of youth are discourses of adolescent psychology and social psychology, which have suggested that adolescence is a destabilizing time of struggle where individuals rely on their peer group to formulate an identity and outwardly express their inward self in a fashion that is both socially acceptable by adults and approved by peers. This affection and acceptance could only be gained and attained (as promised in advertisements) through the continual purchasing of newer, flashier, and prettier consumer goods. This is how perpetual adolescence starts, and why it never ends.

The point then is *not* to suggest that advertising is manipulative or that we have no choice in consuming products and that we are merely sheep being herded by the culture industry. Likewise, the point was not to provide credence to Neil Postman's 1994 claim that childhood has disappeared.[5] Instead this chapter looked at the representations of sexualized youth in contemporary culture, and in particular in advertisements by Abercrombie & Fitch. What was discovered was that it is the fears and anxieties of adults in a society that are reflected in discourses about childhood and it is the hopes, dreams, and desires of adults in a society that are reflected in the advertisements of youth. We still can't get past the Romantic/Puritan dichotomy in representing youth in the media and that has its roots as far back as John Locke and his discussion of the blank slate in the 1690s. Discussion surrounding advertisements of Abercrombie & Fitch continue the debate as to whether we are a society that is in love with our children or at war with them. The consequence of our inability to move past this debate and dichotomy of representation of youth is the continual practice of the marketing discourse of perpetual adolescence and the continual denial of the civil and political rights of children and adults. The marketing discourse of perpetual adolescence denies children civil and political rights by either suggesting that they are incapable of being active participants in politics and in need of protection, or that that they are innocent and should not be taken away from childhood to deal with what are considered adult matters. Equally disturbing is how the marketing discourse of perpetual adolescence denies adults civil and political rights by placing the emphasis of adult life on either the consumption of youthful sensibilities or the protection of children from adult evils instead of the larger issues of injustice and inequality in the world.

Notes

1. The research for the chapter began as a part of my doctoral thesis, and as such, a portion of this article first appears in chapter 2 of *Selling Youth: How Market Research at the J. Walter Thompson Company Framed What It Meant to be a Child (and an Adult) in 20th Century America.* Diss., McGill University, 2008. Montreal: 2008. Print.

2. Adolescence was deemed by psychologists such as G. Stanley Hall and Sigmund Freud to be a time of turbulence, where competing selves needed to be re-organized, where a young person came of age, and where competing sexual urges needed to be controlled in order to function properly in society. With this, adolescence became defined as

a period of destabilization and adolescents became categorized as individuals in need of guidance.

3. Here, the term "culture industries" is used in a similar fashion to how Theodor Adorno and Max Horkheimer use the term in *The Dialectic of Enlightenment* to refer to all of the industries involved in the appropriation and depoliticizing of art, through its mass production and selling for profit.

4. The categories of age and development that such terms associate with childhood are social constructions that have become so widely used and represented that they have become what Stuart Hall would call "naturalized codes." Following Louis Althusser's ideas of "obviousness" and Antonio Gramsci's explanation of how ideology is most dangerous when it becomes invisible, such that it is seen as normal, silly, or stupid, Hall uses the term "naturalized codes" to refer to the representation of an ideology that has become so widespread in our culture that we no longer process and analyze the symbol and instead simply accept it at face value. Under this schema, terms like "adolescent," "teenager," "child," and "youth" all represent an implicit ideology that has become so normalized that we no longer see the dangers inherent in them, the structures of power they contain, and the ways in which they not only colonize children but deny them any access to channels of power.

5. In *The Disappearance of Childhood* Postman stated that "American adults want to be parents of children less than they want to be children themselves."(Postman, 138) According to Postman, advancements in information and communication technology in the second half of the twentieth century has caused a re-organization of the life-stages proposed in adolescent psychology. For Postman, "in the television age there are [now only] three [stages]. At one end, infancy; at the other, senility. In between there is what we might call the adult-child" (99).

Works Cited

Associated Press. "Abercrombie & Fitch Obscenity Charge Dropped: Company Says Cops Overreacted When Citing Manager over Mall Poster." MSNBC.msn.com, February 4, 2008. msnbc.msn.com/id/22993326/ns/business-retail/t/abercrombie-fitch-obscenity-charge-dropped/#.T51l0rNSTTo (accessed August 8, 2008).

Bernfeld, Siegfried. "Uber eine Typische Form der Männlichen Pubertät." *Imago 9* (1923): 169–188.

Bhatnagar, Parija. "Abercrombie Kills Its Racy Catalog:." *CNN.com*, December 10, 2003. cnn.com/2003/US/12/10/abercrombie.catalog/index.html?iref=allsearch (accessed April 29, 2012).

Blos, Peter. *The Adolescent Passage: Developmental Issues*. New York: International Universities Press, 1979.

Britten, Fleur. "Branding the Magazine World." *New York Times*, February 13, 2008. www.nytimes.com/2008/02/13/style/13iht-rmag.4.10016995.html?pagewanted=all (accessed April 29, 2012).

Denizet-Lewis, Benoit. "The Man behind Abercrombie & Fitch." Salon.com, January 24, 2006. salon.com/2006/01/24/jeffries (accessed August 8, 2008).

Duke University Library. *Inventory of the Abercrombie & Fitch Quarterly Catalog Collection, 1997-2007* (accessed August 8, 2008).

Elliot, Stuart. "Abercrombie & Fitch Extends a Print Campaign to TV." *New York Times*, August 6, 1999. nytimes.com/1999/08/06/business/the-media-business-advertising-abercrombie-fitch-extends-a-print-campaign-to-tv.html (accessed August 8, 2008).

Freud, Sigmund. "Three Essays on the Theory of Sexuality." In *The Essentials of Psycho*, edited and translated by J. Strachey, 277–375. London: The Hogarth Press and Institute of Psycho-Analysis, 1986.

Gennaro, Stephen. "Purchasing the Teenage Canadian Identity: ICTs, American Media, and Brand Name Consumption." *International Social Science Review* 80, no. 3 & 4 (2005): 119–136.

———. "Sex & the City: Perpetual Adolescence Gendered Feminine." *Nebula* 4, no. 3 (2007): 246–275..

———. *Selling Youth: How Market Research at the J. Walter Thompson Company Framed What It Meant to be a Child (and an Adult) in 20th Century America*. Diss. Montreal: McGill University, 2008.

Grossberg, Lawrence. *Caught in the Crossfire: Kids, Politics, and America's Future: Cultural Politics and the Promise of Democracy*. Boulder, CO: Paradigm Publishers, 2005.

Hall, G. Stanley. *Adolescence: Its Psychology and Its Relations to Physiology, Anthropology, Sociology, Sex, Crime, Religion and Education*. New York: D. Appleton and Company, 1904.

Hendrick, Harry. "Constructions and Reconstructions of British Childhood: An Interpretative Survey, 1880 to the Present." In *Constructing and Reconstructing Childhood*, edited by Allison James and Alan Prout, 35–39. London: Falmer Press, 1990.

Jenkins, Henry. "Introduction: Childhood Innocence and Other Modern Myths." In *The Children's Culture Reader*, edited by H. Jenkins, 1–37. New York: New York University, 1998.

Johnson, Richard. "Topless Teens." *New York Post*, March 27, 2008. www.nypost.com/p/pagesix/item_EVDPxjtUT2WAmgHTy1z6pJ (accessed August 8, 2008).

Locke, John. "Some Thoughts Concerning Education (1692)." *Fordham University Internet Modern History Sourcebook*. www.fordham.edu/halsall/mod/1692locke-education.asp (accessed April 29, 2012).

Males, Mike. *The Scapegoat Generation: America's War on Adolescents*. Monroe, ME.: Common Courage Press, 1996.

McCullough, Kevin. "Abercrombie & Fitch to Your Kids: Group Sex Now!" *World Net Daily*, 14 Nov. 2003. www.wnd.com/2003/11/2175 (accessed April 29, 2012).

Moschis, George. "Gerontographics: A Scientific Approach to Analyzing and Targeting the Mature Market." *The Journal of Services Marketing* 6.3 (1992): 17–27.

Postman, Neal. *The Disappearance of Childhood*. New York: Vintage Books, 1994.

Reines, Dan. "The Abercrombie & Fitch Catalog Index." Nerve.com, June 11, 2002. nerve.com/regulars/quickies/abercrombieindex (page has become unavailable, April 29, 2012; unarchived).

Rousseau, John. J. *Emile (1762)*. Columbia University Institute for Learning Technologies. ilt.columbia.edu/pedagogies/rousseau (accessed April 29, 2012).

Sammond, Nicholas. *Babes in Tomorrowland: Walt Disney and the Marketing of the American Child, 1930-1960*. Durham: Duke University Press, 2005.

Sarland, Charles. "The Impossibility of Innocence: Ideology, Politics, and Children's Literature." In *Understanding Children's Literature: Key Essays from the Interna-*

tional Companion Encyclopedia of Children's Literature, edited by P. Hunt, 39–55.
    London: Routledge, 1999.
Shani, David, and Sujana Chalasani."Exploiting Niches Using Relationship Marketing."
    The Journal of Business & Industrial Marketing 8.4 (1993):58-67.
Sprinthall, Norman, and W.A. Collins. *Adolescent Psychology: A Developmental View.*
    3rd ed. New York: McGraw-Hill, 1995.
Trend Hunter Magazine. "Magalogue: The Return of Abercrombie & Fitch
    Quarterly." February 22, 2008 (accessed April 29, 2012).

Chapter Four
Configuring Childhood on the Web
by Katie Elson Anderson

It is said that childhood is a journey, not a race. In the days before digital media, portions of this journey were documented for preservation and shared with family and friends. While most of the videos during this time were of special occasions such as birthdays and vacations, technological changes began to increase the ease and frequency in which these memories could be created. Parents began to capture both the entertaining and the mundane, sharing images of their children with an expanding audience, making private moments more public. Digital media continues to change this preservation and sharing quite dramatically, increasing the amount of footage taken, and the potential for expanding to a large, global audience. The video sharing site YouTube provides parents with a platform in which to share moments from their child's journey with a broad audience that was unreachable just a few years ago.

Countless numbers of amateur videos involving children being children, from the bizarre to the mundane are at this moment being uploaded and shared on YouTube. Some of these videos become extremely popular with millions of views while other videos are only clicked on by proud grandparents. Children in these videos become instant celebrities as the images become viral and spread throughout the virtual landscape. In looking at this relatively new phenomenon of sharing images of childhood publicly on the web many questions arise regarding the privacy of the children, motivation of the parents/guardian and the impact on the children and society as a whole. While there is some professional content available on YouTube, this chapter will focus on the user generated content that makes up the majority of the videos uploaded to the site. This chapter will look at why these videos are being shared, why they are being viewed by millions and possible effects that all this sharing has on children, parents and society.

society.

There is an ever increasing presence of amateur videos of children on YouTube. These range from videos of babies falling out of their crib (over 3000) to a father climbing into a child's crib to help the child sleep. In the over 80 percent of amateur videos that are uploaded to YouTube children are heavily represented. Previously, home video-sharing was for the entertainment, amusement, (often) boredom of family and friends; today's videos of children, particularly those of babies, are being made widely available by parents and guardians for the entertainment and amusement of the masses on the Internet. This chapter looks at the evolution, motivation and consequences of this expanded sharing as well as exploring why these videos are so popular with the masses.

Broadcast Yourself

Amateur videos were being viewed and shared well before YouTube came on the scene. Even when YouTube was released in June 2005, it was not the only site providing this service. Prior to video-sharing sites, videos were shared primarily through e-mail, blogs, and social networking sites such as MySpace and Facebook. Entrepreneurs saw a need for a simple and easy way to share the videos that were becoming more and more ubiquitous with the emergence of accessible video creation technologies. The founders of YouTube, Chad Hurley, Steve Chen and Jawed Karim, found success creating a simple and streamlined way for the average person to share videos by uploading to a specific site using keywords and tagging for organization and identification. Burgess and Green provide several different stories regarding how and why YouTube surpassed the competition and became the most popular site for video sharing.[1] However this was achieved, YouTube's popularity caught the eye of Google, and in 2006 Google purchased the site for 1.65 billion dollars.

YouTube's numbers have grown exponentially as more and more users create and share content that is viewed on a number of different platforms (mobile devices such as smartphones, tablets, laptops, PC's etc.). YouTube's tagline is "Broadcast Yourself" and indeed, the numbers prove that is exactly what people are doing. The digital measuring company comScore, Inc. reported that as of April 2011, YouTube had 142.7 million unique users in the United States.[2] YouTube's own statistics page reports that 70 percent of their traffic comes from outside of the United States, so comScore's number is only a small portion of the 800 million unique visitors reported by YouTube on its own statistics page.[3]

These unique users are uploading more than sixty hours of video every minute and this content is being viewed at an increase of 50 percent over last year, with four billion video views a day.[4] The company continues to make improvements such as providing videos in HD and allowing users to upload longer and larger content than when the site was first available. The word "YouTube" itself has become a verb in the same way Google became a verb, people will tell someone to "just YouTube it." Even with other video-sharing sites attempting to contend with YouTube, all indicators point to a continued growth of both users and content.

As YouTube gained recognition and reputation, it became more and more embedded in popular culture with people "YouTubing" on a more regular basis, educators and scholars began to take note. Beyond the wealth of content to be used or examined for instruction and research lie the social community and the impact that this website has had on the world. The site is not just about sharing video that is often low in technical quality but high in emotion and creativity, but about responding to the videos with the same passion and creativity. The participatory structure of the site allows for engaging conversation among members and the general audience through comments or video responses. The fact that so many videos of amateur quality garner the amount of attention and elicit the numbers of responses is intriguing for those in the fields of social sciences. Scholarly literature on YouTube is sparse, but growing. The literature includes exploration of its application in education, privacy issues, and relevancy in film, media and communication studies, political use, and impact to society and culture as a whole.

Michael Wesch, anthropology professor at Kansas State University, uses YouTube to teach and for research. In 2008, he presented "An Anthropological Introduction to YouTube" to the Library of Congress.[5] In his talk, he refers to the work done by the Kansas State University Digital Ethnography research team regarding the content on the site. At the time of the research in March 2008, there were 78.3 million videos on YouTube.[6] Using the same search method as the research team, which was a wild-card search ("*"), provides results of over 500 million. From a nearly random sample of one day's worth of the "Most Recent" videos, the team found that 80.3 percent were user generated, amateur content. YouTube no longer has an option to view the videos by "Most Recent," but filtering the wild-card search to just one day's upload indicates that this percentage has probably changed very little, perhaps with slightly less user-generated content due to an increase in commercial use of YouTube (movie trailers, ads, etc.).

YouTube provides a place to upload, store and most importantly, quickly and easily share this user-generated content. Users can send the link via e-mail, instant message, or post the link to a forum, listserv, or social website. Technology also allows a user to embed the video directly within their own site (Facebook, blogs, other social networking sites etc.) in order to share with their social network. While it is against the terms of agreement, it is also possible to simply lift the video content from YouTube and place it directly on one's own sites. This intense sharing of a particular item can lead to so many mentions, shares and instances of the item on the web that it's spreading becomes "viral." A viral video is a video that becomes so enormously popular through this ease of sharing that it eventual enters the consciousness of mainstream popular culture. Many viral videos have become legendary with Wikipedia entries, fan sites, and references in television shows, movies and throughout the Internet. Oftentimes, a viral video, or part of it (clip, screenshot, catchphrase) will also become an Internet meme, or Internet phenomenon and further solidify its iconic place in popular culture. Viral videos existed well before YouTube, but YouTube has allowed for the perpetuation of previous viral videos, faster spreading of new viral videos and responses to these media. In discussing the phenomenon that is YouTube, Wesch gives an excellent description of this phenomenon in his explanation of how the video "NumaNuma" spread to become one of the most viewed videos of all time with an estimated 700 million in 2006.[7] Estimating the number of views of pre-YouTube videos is not an easy task, given the far-reaching qualities of Internet sharing. Even now, the amount of views listed on YouTube is not completely accurate, as videos can be reproduced and posted in other locations that are not linked to the statistics. Tracking views and ranking viral videos is easier and more accurate now that there is the centralized location of YouTube. Lists have been generated to rank the most popular videos on YouTube and several videos with images of children appear on these lists. In fact, the most popular user generated video on YouTube is a video of two children.[8] The video, "Charlie Bit My Finger—Again!"[9] is a less-than-one-minute video of one-year-old Charlie and three-year-old Harry and has been viewed over 394 million times, making it the most viewed amateur video. While no other images of children have reached the amount of views as this one, several have reached millions of hits and garnered much publicity and attention for the children involved. It is apparent in the many lists and charts on YouTube content, that children, specifically laughing babies and precocious toddlers, are quite popular with the viewing population.

The Evolution of Home Video

Before Charlie bit Harry, the most viewed video of all time in August 2007 was "The Evolution of Dance"[10] by comedian Judson Laipply. This video is a six-minute montage which shows the evolution of dance from 1956 to the present by showcasing popular songs and dance moves. The dance moves flow from one to the other into one seamless move that covers a broad spectrum of physical movement to music. In much the same way, the evolution of home movies and video spans this time period, adapting to changing society and technology while creating cultural images.

Societal changes have always influenced the use of technology–and in the case of home movies–increasing numbers of children played a major role. In looking at the history of amateur film, Zimmerman points out that post World War II's increased birthrates led to more and bigger nuclear families. This, along with larger amounts of leisure time and less expensive equipment for making amateur film resulted in the creation of more home movies. Evidence of the popularity of home movie creation is found in the tips and how-to's that appear in both photography magazines of the time and in family and parenting magazines.[11] Children and babies in particular have always been a focus of home movies as parents attempt to capture the moments and document the fast changes that take place in infancy. As equipment for making these home movies became less expensive and more accessible, more families were able to capture the important moments in their child's lives. The cost of film remained low enough that these families could make the films, but was still high enough as to only warrant special occasions; birthdays, weddings, holidays, and so on. Amateur film-making equipment, such as the 8 mm camera, became ubiquitous in the middle-class homes of America, and remained an important part of childhood up until the 1980s with the introduction of video cameras for the home.

The introduction of video cameras changed the way family memories were recorded. Video was less expensive, had longer recording times and was easier to maintain and operate. Instead of reserving the recording for special events, families were able to record more mundane, everyday life events. Video provided more portability, both for the film-maker and for the finished product as VHS tapes could be created, copied and sent to relatives in the mail.

Video technology has changed quite a bit since its first introduction to the home in 1981. With the shift to digital it became faster, smarter, and smaller. Video cameras decreased in size, digital cameras were given video capabilities and now, it is difficult to find a cell phone without video capabilities. Much of today's video creation takes place on devices that fit in someone's pocket. webcams, available on just about every new computer, have changed the face of home video as well, eliminating the need for another person to record.

About a decade after the introduction of the video camera, a market emerged for home mode images. According to Pini, the term "home mode" is used to describe material that deals primarily with the home, material that is domestic and familial, and in most cases private.[12] Moran discusses how these private images went public with the introduction of reality-based television and the appearance of home videos on television.[13] The most popular place for home video on television was *America's Funniest Home Videos*,[14] where viewers submitted their home mode videos for the chance to be on television and perhaps even win an award for having recorded the most humorous event. During an episode of *America's Funniest Home Videos*, a studio audience voted on the "best" video. The modern-day version of this is YouTube, with the audience able to give a "thumbs-up" or a "thumbs-down" and comment on the videos that have been submitted.

Throughout the technological changes, children have always been an important part of the home mode of image creation. Implied in the definition of home mode is that it exists in the private sphere, rather than a public sphere.[15]

Studies on amateur film by Zimmerman and Moran, however, were written well before private and public life merged on the Internet. When home movies moved from film to video they were more easily shared, expanding the audience well beyond the nuclear family. VHS tapes could be copied and mailed, providing greater distribution of the images. A move to digital exponentially increased the audience, with the ability to e-mail and share on social networking sites, firmly placing home video in the public sphere. What would once have been restricted to just family and friends is now being offered to anyone with an Internet connection via video-sharing sites like YouTube. The ability to share media has also transformed with each new technology, allowing for greater dispersion of the mundane and everyday events of a person's life.

The ease with which a home video can be created via cell phones, tablets, and small camcorders allows parents to capture moments in their children's lives that would not previously have been recorded via the more formal methods of home video. Many videos available on YouTube involve the happenstance recording of an entertaining or significant moment in children's lives. Parents are able to record minute after minute of insignificant moments in the hopes of capturing one significant one. Sometimes that moment can be very entertaining, and when shared with a wider audience becomes extremely popular. With immense popularity and a strong presence in popular culture, this moment becomes significant not just to the child being taped but to society as a whole.

Broadcast Your Kids

Announcing the birth of a child via picture message or by posting a picture on a social network has become commonplace. Many newborn pictures appear in the virtual world within minutes of the child's appearing in the physical world. In many cases, this picture of their first few minutes is not the first time they are appearing online, with many people posting ultrasound pictures to announce a pregnancy. In a study conducted by Internet security firm AVG it was found that 23 percent of parents share images from prenatal sonograms on the web.[16] In August 2011, Facebook made it easier for couples to share the news by adding "expected child" to their list of friends and family.[17] Whether the presence begins before or after birth, the AVG study determined that 92 percent of children in the U.S. have an online presence by the time they are two.[18] An online presence is considered to range from photos shared by parents to individual social networking profiles. Children have become integral parts of their parents' online lives and, more recently, have begun to have their own separate online presence through posts on blogs, social networks and sharing sites, including YouTube. These pictures, descriptions and videos become a permanent part of a child's web presence and follow these children as they grow older, creating a virtual baby book for all to see.

Unlike the baby books, old films and VHS tapes that chronicled a child's life, these virtual pieces of a child's life do not end up on dusty shelves or in basement boxes. Instead, they are forever being archived on servers and in some cases distributed to many different online locations. With the ease of creating, uploading and sharing video, the percentage of a child's life that is publicly available on the Internet will continue to increase. When today's two-year-olds turn thirty, most of their lives will have been chronicled in some virtual fashion. As children get older, they take over the role of creating and posting content with or without their parents' permission and/or knowledge. While many social networking sites set minimum age limits for account holders, there is proof that both children and parents are finding ways around these restrictions.[19]

Whether uploaded by the families of the children, or the children themselves, vast quantities of videos with images of children are being uploaded to YouTube every day. A search on the term "babies" results in over 28,000 videos. Not all of these videos involve human babies or are home videos, but the majority of those scrolled through are amateur video of babies laughing maniacally, dancing, singing, being born and even breast-feeding. It would be close to impossible to quantify an exact percentage of amateur videos containing images of children, as this would require a more complete inventory and evaluation of YouTube content than this chapter allows. A quick glance at the videos being uploaded in a single day does provide some insight. Searching on popular tags that appear in some of the viral videos and filtering to "today" for three days provided the following information. With an average of 30,000 videos uploaded, there were approximately: 500 were tagged "baby laughing;" 500 tagged "baby singing;" and an average of 700 tagged "funny kid." Also of note is the fact that out of the top 50 most viral videos in 2010, seven involved images of children.[20]

Is This Real Life?

As previously mentioned, the top-viewed user-generated content on YouTube is the video "Charlie Bit Me—Again!" The video was uploaded in May 2007 by the children's parents in Great Britain in order to be viewed by relatives in the United States.[21] This fifty-six-second clip captures two young siblings at play. One year-old Charlie bites the finger of three-year-old Harry while Harry patiently allows this to happen. Harry exclaims to the camera that "Charlie bit him." He then places his finger back in his younger brother's mouth while Charlie bites him again. As it is happening, Harry exclaims in his British accent, "Ouch, Charlie . . . ouch," while his younger brother continues to clamp down on the finger. Harry then admonishes his brother by saying, "Ouch, Charlie, that really hurt," and Charlie turns and laughs. Charlie continues to laugh while Harry tells the camera that "Charlie bit me and that really hurt." The video shows the patience of an older brother and the innocence of childhood play. The

facial contortions of Harry as his brother continues to bite him despite his holler-
ing combined with Charlie's laughter makes for an amusing moment. For many,
the British accent ads to the appeal. Without a doubt it is an amusing moment in
the lives of these two boys, but there are certainly thousands of humorous moments available on YouTube. It is difficult to explain how and why certain videos garner the attention that they do. In this case, the website CollegeHumor.com,
a comedic content sharing site featured this video, catapulting it into the lime-
light.[22] Once it went viral, the video elicited so many responses, parodies, dedi-
cations and remixes that there is actually an entire website dedicated to these,
charliebit.me.

Another early viral video was is "Laughing Baby,"[23] also known as
"Hahaha." The camera focuses on a baby laughing hysterically at the sounds
being made from off camera. This video captures the pure unadulterated joy of
baby laughter. The original has been removed due to copyright claims, but not
before it too was copied, remixed and repurposed. This video was the first in a
very long line of viral laughing babies. One could spend days immersed in the
laughter of babies available on YouTube. Several other videos capturing the joy
of laughter and discovery have become quite popular with the YouTube community and have spread into Internet memes. None of these children have
gained the cyber celebrity status of Harry and Charlie, whose family continues
to share some moments publicly, eventually including a third child, Jasper.

One child who has gained recognition as a YouTube star is David from
"David after Dentist."[24] The video "David after Dentist" was uploaded in January of 2009 and shows seven-year-old David after visiting the dentist for a procedure. He is still under the influence of the drugs and his father is taping him as
he sits in his car seat while he tells the camera that he feels funny and then begins to worry that he will be like that forever, turning philosophical and asking
"Is this real life?" before trying to get out of his car seat while screaming at the
top of his lungs. When this video appeared on that scene, it prompted some
questions regarding children's images in public space. The video can be uncom-
fortable to watch as it is a child in a vulnerable position of distress and confusion. While the child's behavior can be seen by some as entertaining, it is not
surprising that many have questioned the appropriateness of sharing this moment in David's life. Many others have expressed concern for David and questioned his parents' motives for making the video public, despite the father's as-
sertion that it was originally uploaded in order for David's mother to see that he
was OK after the procedure.[25] The question of motive is a pressing one when
looking at the hundreds of thousands of images of children available on
YouTube. Parents are uploading images of their children at an astonishing rate,
exposing private moments to a world-wide audience.

In the earlier days of viral videos, motive was not questioned as much as it
is now. When Charlie and David were uploaded, it was readily assumed that a
parent unwittingly posted a private moment for the consumption of friends and

family only to find out the video had been "discovered." However, the possibility of discovery has now become more of a competition than a happenstance. It is not possible to talk about YouTube and discovery without mentioning the most beloved and hated music celebrity, Justin Bieber. In 2007, Justin Bieber was one of thousands of children on YouTube performing for a home camera. His mother uploaded the videos of him singing in a bathroom mirror and performing at local talent shows in order to share them with friends and family.[26] His story is legendary because his videos began to get views outside of family and friends and eventually were viewed by a promoter and music manager. This led to recording contracts and eventually his current status as a mega star. Justin Bieber is evidence that it is possible to move beyond the fifteen minutes of fame and millions of views on YouTube and into the mainstream music scene. It seems that now everybody is uploading their children singing, in the hopes of being the next Justin Bieber. In many cases these videos and the children in them do achieve momentary stardom, being featured on talk shows, websites and the newscasts. However, so far no one has come close to capitalizing on their YouTube stardom like Justin Bieber.

Children by nature are entertaining. Their laughter is contagious and their dance moves are to be reckoned with. Art Linkletter and Bill Cosby highlighted for television audiences that kids do "say the darndest things." Even the inadvertent mispronunciation of words can lead to laughable, albeit inappropriate, situations. All of these moments are being captured on YouTube. From a young boy telling his mother that he only likes her when she gives him cookies to a child being prompted to say, "fire truck" without the correct pronunciation, the everyday lives of children and their parents are becoming a huge part of popular culture. From kitchen tables to car seats, the images of children in their daily lives that used to be shared in a small community of friends and family are now available to the world. This exposure to the entire on-line world can be cause for some questions and concern regarding the child's privacy and protection as well as questions regarding the parent's motivation for sharing the image and the subsequent capitalization of the image.

Privacy and Protection

Privacy

It is difficult to avoid the word "privacy" when discussing the Internet and social networking sites. The staggering amount of personal data that is collected by websites, particularly social networking sites has been cause for some concern. The lines between public and private are blurred, with younger generations unaware even of the invasion to their privacy that is taking place.. There would be no cause for discussion of the public images of children if their parents had chosen to keep their videos private.

When videos of children go viral, the parents often contend that when they uploaded the video, they did not intend it for public viewership, but instead wanted to share it with family and friends.[27] This excuse was accepted in the earlier advent of viral videos, but is currently being met with more skepticism as evidenced by the comments on the YouTube videos and the comments on the articles about these video, with many viewers pointing out how it appears that parents are looking to achieve the fame of the Charlies and Davids. In some cases the parents are simply ignorant of the fact that most defaults on social sharing sites are set to show everyone everything, and are not aware of options for privacy. In other cases, the parent is aware of what needs to be done to keep a video private, but does not take the steps necessary to do so. At times, these steps are confusing and time consuming. Companies like YouTube that profit from the advertising on public videos are certainly not going to make it an easy process. YouTube originally only had two options for sharing, public or private, with the private option being limited to twenty-five users who also had YouTube accounts. In May 2010 YouTube began to offer a third option.[28] The unlisted option was added, allowing users to limit access to include only those individuals who have been provided with a direct link. This obviously makes it much easier to share less publicly as there are no limits to the number of people who can view it and the recipients do not need to have a YouTube account. However, while this hides the video from searching and viewing by anyone, it does not guarantee complete privacy as the link can be shared again by the people with whom you shared the video.

It is in YouTube's best interest to have all videos available to the public as more videos viewed equals more money from advertising. YouTube recommends that content be shared this way. Despite this, the site does include instructions on how to keep videos private. The Community Guidelines discuss the importance of exercising caution when posting images of children:. "Please be cautious when posting something involving a child. If you're sharing a private moment or home movie, consider making it a private video so that only your family and friends can see it."[29]

Most of the users uploading videos have probably not found their way to these pages or even to the Privacy Notice which informs the user that videos submitted to YouTube may be redistributed and viewed by the general public and all information can be collected and used by others.[30] By agreeing to the terms of service a user should also be aware that they granting every other user a non-exclusive license to access their content and to "use, reproduce, distribute, display and perform such content."[31] Essentially, when a video is uploaded to YouTube, the owner of the video should be aware that the content can be viewed, shared, reproduced, repurposed, and displayed by just about anyone.

If parents and guardians are ignorant of the privacy settings or not taking the time and effort to make their videos private, it can be assumed that they are also unaware of the notices and terms that allow these videos to be distributed widely and used. In fact, some comments by the parents themselves illustrate a lack of understanding that they have for all practical purposes ceded anything but ownership and ownership is not often respected in the online world of rampant theft and plagiarism. Not only do television and news shows use these videos, but other YouTube users steal them and upload them to their own channels and also repurpose and remix them without the owner's needing to give permission or determine if it is proper (and in some cases it is most definitely not proper).

Protection

Once a video has gone viral, an owner's control of the image and what is said about it is largely out of their hands. The concerns go beyond just the posting and viewing of the videos, given the participatory nature of YouTube. Users are encouraged to comment on the videos and as Lev Grossman summed it up: "Some of the comments on YouTube make you weep for the future of humanity just for the spelling alone, never mind the obscenity and the naked hatred."[32] Videos with images of children are not exempt from this obscenity and naked hatred. While most of the comments on the higher-viewed videos of children are positive, there are usually inappropriate and obscene comments that are racist, sexist, misogynistic, homophobic and hateful. There are racist remarks on every ethnic child's video that was viewed by the author and personal attacks on both the children and the parents on all other videos. While these comments are disturbing, it is refreshing to see that there is a certain amount of policing done by the YouTube community with users confronting those who comment inappropriately, but at times it appears that it is hard for the community to keep up with those who wish to spread their vitriol.

As with privacy, there are ways to control the commenting content that appears with a child's image, but it does appear that few users are either aware of these or willing to take the time and effort to reduce the hateful words. The default for comments is to "allow comments automatically," which appears to be the setting that most people use when a video is first uploaded. The obvious choice for avoiding any negative comments would be to not allow comments at all. This, however, is antithetical to the nature of YouTube and is not always well received by the community as it is essentially shutting down the social aspect of the social networking site. There is a setting to approve comments, which is of course quite time consuming with videos that have millions of viewers and thousands of comments. As an example, "Charlie Bit Me—Again!" does allow comments with a plea from the parents to keep them family friendly. It does appear that the comments are being monitored by the owner of the video.

Comments are one thing that can be controlled when the necessary precautions are taken in order to protect the child's image. What is almost impossible to control is the redistribution, reuse and repurposing of the images. As the privacy notice states, any video that is submitted to YouTube may be redistributed through the Internet and other media channels. Many parents have naively stated that they can simply remove a video in order to protect their child. However, simply removing the original video does not always remove all impressions of it on the Internet. For example "Laughing Baby," the original video that went viral has been removed with a copyright claim. However, there are so many copies still available that the baby's laughter continues to entertain. In many cases, the video is redistributed and reused so often, it is difficult to determine the original source. Not only does the video appear throughout YouTube, but it can appear outside of YouTube. Even when the actual video is not used, there are images, screenshots and portions of the video being distributed. Once a video is uploaded publicly, there is really no way to control when and how it appears throughout the Internet and other media.

Many YouTube videos do appear on other media, from local newscasts to late-night television. The immense popularity of these user generated videos has spawned television shows dedicated to viral videos such as *Web Soup* and *Tosh.0*. Talk show hosts Ellen Degeneres and Tyra Banks often highlight and even interview the latest YouTube star, and late night host Jimmy Kimmel encourages parents to post videos of their children reacting to his suggestions to lie or trick them. Parents have uploaded videos of their children's reactions to being told all of their Halloween candy has been eaten and opening terribly disappointing Christmas presents, like half-eaten sandwiches. [33] In many cases where video content is featured on television shows, viewers are encouraged to submit their own content in order to participate in the conversation about videos.

In the cases of *Web Soup*, *Tosh.0* and *Jimmy Kimmel Live!* the content of the television show is adult in nature. When the videos of children are featured in this medium, oftentimes the comments, jokes and discussion surrounding the video are not always child friendly. Parents should be aware that when they are posting videos without privacy restrictions, they are exposing their children to an audience beyond the already expansive YouTube viewership. In many cases, the appearance of a video on one of these shows has further established a video's place in popular culture. An example of this is Rebecca Black's "Friday," [34] which was mentioned on the *Tosh.0* blog and tweeted about by a comedian in a negative fashion, criticizing both the songwriting and the performance of the song. These two events have been credited with thrusting the teenage Rebecca Black into the spotlight, though not necessarily in a positive light. [35] The effects of this ironic popularity amounted to the bullying of a teenager by countless adults who commented on the blog, the tweets, their social media sites and the video itself.

The public and participatory nature of YouTube along with the anonymity of the Internet is a recipe for bullying. One of the most viral videos, even said to be the most viewed video of all time, "The Star Wars Kid" is actually one of the first cases of cyber-bullying, as it was the classmates of fifteen-year-old Ghyslian Raza who uploaded the video that he had mistakenly left in school video equipment.[36] An extreme case of bullying of children by peers and adults that played out via YouTube and other participatory websites is the case of Jessica Leonhardt, aka Jessi Slaughter, an eleven- year-old who, according to Gawker, was beaten up by the Internet.[37] In a response to some harassment taking place on a social media site, Jessi posted a YouTube video in which she tries to act older than her eleven-year-old self and makes violent threats against her haters. This YouTube video was then shared on other social media sites, 4chan and tumblr. One could argue that the response to her video was hateful, invasive and disturbing. Not only was she bullied and harassed on the sites, but users went so far as to post her personal information and take the harassment to non-virtual heights. While her videos show an adolescent in great distress, her questionable decisions and behaviors should not have warranted adult attacks on any eleven-year-old.

While the saga of Jessi Slaughter is an extreme case, the images of children that are uploaded to YouTube are not safe from direct insults in the comments, features on shows containing adult humor or even reimaging in inappropriate ways. There are many examples of the viral videos of children being repurposed with inappropriate content, thus pairing the children's image with adult themes and language. In seeing what is being done with the images of children, one wonders why parents choose to upload their children's images or allow their children to upload their own images.

My Child's Video Has One Million Hits on YouTube

While this bumper sticker has yet to be seen, it is probably not a far stretch to imagine its existence. As we look at the issues of privacy and protection, questions arise as to the motivation for publicly sharing one's private videos. Internet fame and celebrity has exploded in recent years and YouTube can take a lot of the credit as it churns out viral video stars on what seems to be a weekly basis. As evidenced in previous articles on the viral celebrities, many of the parents who suddenly found their children thrust into the spotlight proclaim that they were uploading videos only to share with friends and family. At times, though, it appears that the motivation is not always this innocent. The potential for discovery and fame is often hard to resist. There are books and websites that instruct on how to increase views, create viral content and promote videos.[38] Some of these tactics involve tagging, which is a way of cataloging the video with keyword terms for discoverability. There is a popular practice of adding tags for the sole purpose of attracting viewers. For example, several videos of "funny kids" contain tags referring to "Charlie Bit Me," or other heavily viewed videos so

anyone searching for these popular items would possibly find the video. An example of one that has been tagged with words to increase hits is "Emerson—
Mommy's Nose is Scary."[39] This video has been tagged with "Charlie Bit My
Finger," "Bill O'Reilly," "Perez Hilton" and other terms that are not related to
the content of the video. Other ways to promote one's video include pointing to
the video from other websites such as blogs, social networking sites and other
aggregators.[40]

The potential for a child to become a celebrity through YouTube may be
creating a new type of stage parent, one who uploads the images and works to
spread their videos to as many viewers as possible. As the popularity of images
of children increases, so too does the number of videos being uploaded. There is
a competition for viewership and an inflated sense of celebrity to be attained.
The motivation for increasing views of a video goes beyond the fame and potential celebrity status as there is actually profit to be made on the images.

YouTube's Partner Program is a revenue-sharing program through which
users can earn money from their original content. Essentially, users earn money
from the ads that are placed on the content and the amount of money is based on
the number of views. YouTube provides some promotion and advice on optimi-
zation. The exact specifications of the Partner Program are available on the
YouTube website and explain in further detail the relationship between the ads,
YouTube and the user. There are examples of individuals who are actually making a living off of this partnership.[41,42]

One of these partners, ShayCarl, makes over $140,000 by vlogging, or vid-
eo logging, the daily activities of his family, which includes his four children
With close to one million subscribers, his videos, many of which include his
children have been viewed over 400 million times.[43] The profits made from multiple YouTube channels allow ShayCarl to stay home with his children and
make a living off of YouTube.[44]

Unlike these partners, the average user who uploads videos to be viewed by
friends and family is unlikely to qualify for this program. YouTube, however, is
not one to miss out on potential revenue, and the company takes note of users
whose videos go viral and invites these users to become part of the Individual
Video Program (IVP). This program allows the average person to profit from a
viral video.

Parents can add to the IVP revenue through promotion, merchandising and
licensing. David DeVore, father of "David after Dentist" was able to quit his job
in real estate in order to create a business around the video, earning over
$100,000 in merchandising and licensing.[45] The parents of Charlie and Harry
have made over $150,000.[46] Companies are now turning to YouTube for adver-
tising content, paying parents for the use of their children's images. According
to *The New York Times*, Gerber recently released an ad campaign using "Charlie
Bit Me—Again!" and another viral video "I Don't Like You Mommy."[47] Maxwell House[48] and Hyundai[49] are also using YouTube stars for current advertising

content and there have been speculations that Disney will be paying for the rights to a six year-old's reaction to finding out she is going to Disney.[50]

In many cases the parents speak of the money going to college funds or charity. For example, David DeVore has donated over $6,000 of the profits to charity.[51] Where there is money to be made off of the images of children, there is and always has been controversy. The questions that rise with these YouTube stars are the same questions that have been asked regarding children's images in photography and child stars on television. These questions include moral and ethical implications of exploiting children for profit. Unlike photographs and television, however, content on YouTube has a greater reach and a longer shelf life, and thus is more likely to affect the children and their future selves.

Exploit Your Kids?

When a parent chooses to upload their child's image to YouTube, in many cases the child is too young to grant permission, even if she or he had been asked. When we explore the images of children on YouTube, ethical questions arise as to the appropriateness of parents creating an online presence for their child or putting their children in a potential spotlight. Once that child has achieved celebrity status more questions are posed when that popularity is used for profit. Beyond the ethical question of whether a child would want his or her image to be shared, the fact that these videos are amateur presents legal issues involving legal protection and taxes. Child actors are protected by laws such as the Coogan Law, which requires some of the money to be set aside in a trust account for the child.[52] In the United States, there are tax laws regarding the reporting of income and the filing of taxes for children earning money in the entertainment industry.[53] Children in amateur videos are not considered child actors, but once they have gone viral, these children can be considered child stars. Are there protections in place for guaranteeing that they see the revenue being generated from their images? What are the legal implications for when these children reach adulthood? Are they able to sue their parents or even the websites where their images appear?

The question of whether the sharing of private videos for public consumption is exploitation is a common one on mommy blogs and parenting forums. With more and more videos of children going viral and news stories regarding the potential money to be made, this issue sparks much debate and discussion. On one side of the debate are those who feel that there is no harm in earning college funds from a brief and entertaining moment in childhood. Others feel that using one's child for fame and even profit is exploitive. David DeVore in particular is much vilified for his marketing of David's image and words on the website, davidafterdentist.com. The question of exploitation comes up in the comments on the videos, blog posts, and news stories. This topic was recently addressed in an article on CNET[54] which looked at three videos, "David after Dentist," a three year-old's cooking show that was achieving popularity and a disturbing performance of *Scarface* by children which substituted popcorn for cocaine and the word "fudge" for the expletive beginning with the same letter. The article, which also appeared on CNN and was discussed in *The New York Times* looked at the new phenomenon of kid viral videos and their controversial nature. One of the videos discussed was "The Yippity Yo Cooking Show" which featured three-year-old Zaylee Jean. The father who was interviewed talked about the safety of his child and did not disclose his last name. He also stated that should the popularity become an issue, he would not hesitate to remove the video. Interestingly, since the aforementioned article was written in April 2010, both the cooking show and the *Scarface* performance have been removed from YouTube. It would seem that the articles themselves questioning exploitation led to more concerns regarding the privacy and safety of Zaylee Jean. The *Scarface* video has been taken down due to copyright.

Discussions on blogs and news articles address whether posting a video of one's child to YouTube in the hopes of fame and fortune is exploitation or smart college fund planning. It is a difficult question to address, and in most cases, judgment cannot be placed across the board as the effect on the child has for the most part has yet to be determined. David of "David After Dentist" has embraced his fame, appearing on Tosh 2.0 in a "web redemption," [55] giving interviews, and continuing to thrive and profit from his seven year-old self. The mother of "I Don't Like You Mommy" addresses these concerns on the video description, "People have also asked me about the revenue (ad money) that we get. I would like to share that all the YouTube ad money goes into the kids [sic] savings account so they can go to college. I just try and do what's best for my kids and if all this helps them go to a great school then great." [56]

Self-Identity in the Age of Google

When David and Charlie get older and decide to Google themselves, they will be presented with an extraordinary amount of hits. They will find their videos, the parodies of their videos, news stories, blog posts, interviews and references to a particular moment in their childhood. While David and Charlie are obviously extreme cases, it is safe to say that the children of today will be the Google hits of tomorrow. In an age where images, videos and status updates are posted with impunity, today's children will find more information about themselves than any generation before. Childhood memories that were once limited to the scrapbooks and photo albums on the family room shelves are now part of the Internet. Colleges and employers are increasingly using the web to learn more about applicants, and all signs indicate this will continue. What will happen when employers are able to find an entire lifetime of videos for a prospective employee?

Children whose images appear publicly are being robbed of their right to create their own web presence. The Internet is a new frontier with individuals creating their presence through videos, profiles, status updates, comments and responses to others. There is an excitement in being able to carve out one's space on the web through this creation, an excitement that these children will not experience. While this generation is busy creating and maintaining a web presence, future generations will be working to modify and perhaps delete pieces of their on-line identity.

In one of the only sources to discuss images of children on YouTube, Michael Strangelove in his book *Watching YouTube*[57] brings up the fact that the long-term consequences for the generation that is growing up both watching YouTube and being watched on YouTube are largely unknown. He discusses how "we are transforming passing moments of our childhood into moments permanently fixed in global media culture."[58] Strangelove identifies an important point regarding a child's self-perception and how YouTube is increasing the number of people who can influence one's perception of one's self. The widespread exposure of one's childhood leads to more individuals influencing the memory and manipulating intimate memories. In the example of Harry and Charlie, Strangelove states that they "face a future that is partially defined by events of their childhood that have been posted to YouTube, appropriated, and reinterpreted." [59] He goes on to express concern that "we may be creating conditions for self-construction where the past plays a much more current role in our lives."[60] Technology has always changed how family memories are created and preserved, but Strangelove points out, that YouTube could actually be altering how identities are constructed in the public sphere.

As these children face a future that is defined by events of their childhood that have been shared publicly, they also run the risk that not only their self-perception but also their memories of their childhood are being altered by the public sphere. Research on memories and photographs have shown that photographs and pictures can contribute to memory inaccuracies, suggesting that photographs can make people think they experienced something or performed an action that they did not.[61] Also mentioned in this article is the fact that when people are shown video of themselves completing an action, they can falsely believe that they actually did the action. There should be concern for the children whose images are being co-opted by the Internet that their own childhood memories could be altered by viewing manipulated videos of themselves. Fortunately, it has been found that the likelihood of false memories from visual aids is more likely to occur with something plausible[62] so many of the outrageous co-opting of the children's images is less likely to alter their memory, but could still be disturbing and upsetting for their future selves.

iChild

All of these images create a digital footprint for the child growing up under the child growing up under the careful watch of the online world. Like the movie *The Truman Show* that broadcast every minute of Truman's life, these children's life performances are transmitted to a large viewing audience primarily for the purpose of entertainment, with a broad and diverse definition of entertainment.

Much of the discussion in this chapter has focused on the images of children too young to make decisions regarding their public appearance on YouTube. YouTube's terms of service state that a user must be thirteen-years-old in order to sign up. Thus, presumably children under thirteen are not creating and uploading their own content. However as with Facebook[63] there are certainly children under thirteen creating and using YouTube accounts. Also as with Facebook, these accounts are both monitored and unmonitored by the parents. A sampling of videos on YouTube show a twelve-year-old singer whose channel specifically states that it is monitored by her parents, but many others do not appear as if their parents know that they have YouTube accounts much less the type of material being posted.

While this discussion of the controversies and concerns is centered on the images of children under thirteen, it is pertinent to briefly discuss the user-generated content of children thirteen and older. While much of YouTube is filled with images of children created by adults, there is a strong representation of child-created content. According to Strangelove, fourteen-year-old Lucas Cruickshank produced YouTube's first popular weekly series to reach over 1 million subscribers. Lucas's videos feature him performing the character of six-year-old Fred Figglehorn, whose popularity caused the channel to become the fastest growing in YouTube's history. This of course brought Lucas endorsement deals and media attention.[64]

There are many more examples of teenagers who have created videos and channels in order to perform for a larger audience. Singers and songwriters feature both original content and covers. Dancers show their moves on dance floors ranging from their bedroom floors to wedding dance floors. There is seemingly no end to the aspiring actors, singers, songwriters, comedians and dancers who post their material to YouTube in order to share with the world. It is impossible to list the many channels I viewed, though admittedly a favorite is iTr3vor,[65] one of the many teens who dances with reckless abandon in front of a web cam, but in Trevor's case he does it an Apple store, thus highlighting the reactions to his performance by the patrons and employees of the store. While many of the teenagers who upload their videos are promoting themselves in hopes of their fifteen minutes of fame or more, others simply use this venue as a means of self-expression, a venue so public that previous generations did not have, and in some cases would never have dreamed of.

Innocent Gremlins

Historically, images of children have been popular for their depictions of innocence. Angelic babes, chubby cherubs and rosy-cheeked darlings are the images
of the "naturally innocent child," which Higonnet calls the "Romantic child."[66]
These pictures of the Romantic child are full of "dimpled limbs and knuckles,
round cheeks, silken hair, belonging to a timeless utopia."[67] In the explorations
of the history of popular images of children, a major theme is that from paintings to photography, the innocence of children has historically been emphasized
and highlighted in these images. The popularity of these romantic images is,
according to Higonnet, because "they show us what we want childhood to be."[68]
If the most popular paintings and photographs of children have traditionally
been those of innocence, one might expect that the most popular video images of
children would be of those innocent moments in childhood. While some of the
most popular videos could be described in part as depicting a "Romantic child,"
it is safe to say that the majority actually depict a different type of child. Many
of these videos capture moments when the children become what Cross describes as a "Gremlin child."[69] He describes the transformation from the cute
and "ultimately controlled by parents" to the cool—"the opposite of the cuddly
and delightful to parents."[70] Cross describes the shift from cute to cool as children's images became more commercialized and commercialism began to directly engage children. He also explores the contributions of literature, comics,
television and video games to this transition to cool. Cross presents the origins
of the modern Gremlin child, explaining that "children found freedom from the
cute in the liberating danger of the street while parents' encouragement of the
'innocent' urchin and coquette inadvertently led to the violence and sexuality of
the cool."[71] This in some cases perfectly describes the performances of children
that are found on YouTube.

The children in the videos explored in this chapter are cute, cool, Romantic,
innocent and impish. Their performances are entertaining and delightful, yet can
also be viewed as concerning or disturbing. Higonnet proposes that the "movement of photography mounts a solid argument in favor of childhood as great
human subjects which is bound to have its dark and turbulent side. Childhood
has the power to threaten as well as delight."[72] These same words apply to the
movement of home video shared publicly.

Unlike photography and paintings, videos can capture much more than a
single moment in time. They are not limited to one expression of a child. Instead, the videos can capture many different elements of a child. The performances on YouTube capture both the Romantic child and the Gremlin child and
the most popular videos show both. In "Charlie Bit Me—Again!" Harry is the
innocent child while Gremlin Charlie appears at times to gleefully chomp on his
brother's finger. Jake, the child who tells his mother he doesn't always like her,

is the picture of the Romantic child, chubby cheeks, ruddy complexion. However, he tells his mother that he only likes her when she gives him cookies, and becomes more of a gremlin. "My Daughter Has Turned to the Darkside" captures gremlin and innocent in just nine seconds as the child strikes an angelic smile at the end of her destructive wrath and evil laugh. The laughing babies are all cherub-like until they open their mouths and emit what some of the comments describe as "evil" laughter. Paintings and photographs, while able to capture expressions and emote innocence or impishness, have never been able to capture each frame of expression or howl of pleasure at watching a toy car plummet from a table.

Why are these so popular? While society continues to enjoy the romantic pictures of innocent children such as those by photographer Anne Geddes, there is a demand for the Gremlin child on YouTube. These children are embraced for a number of reasons. They are cute, seriously cute. Their cuteness elicit comments like "I want this baby," "my kids better be this awesome," thus inspiring hope and the promise of pro-creation. They are not perfect. The videos capture the best and worst of parenting. Other parents can feel the joy and pain and know that their children are just like others. They make us laugh. It is nearly impossible to resist the contagious laughter of an eight-month-old shrieking in glee at the ripping of paper. Judging by many of the comments, these videos are being viewed multiple times by individuals looking to experience the joy and wonder expressed in these images.

The pace at which these videos are being shared does not seem to be slowing down. As this chapter nears completion, more videos continue to appear. A recent viral video is of an eight-year-old performing her first hardcore song[73] with a link to purchase the single on iTunes, or T-shirts with her image and lyrics. In less than a month, a six-year-olds' response[74] to this video is on its way to also becoming viral, also selling on iTunes. Some, like these appear to be blatant promotions, while others are simply private moments that have inadvertently gone viral. The number of cute kids doing cool things is astonishing. There is a never-ending stream of content, and it only seems to be increasing with each new meme, viral video or child appearing on *The Ellen Degeneres Show*. There appears to be no easing of demand for these videos or the media coverage. The Huffington Post encourages parents to send videos of their children, and reports on the viral videos. The popularity, content and backstory of these videos have become nightly news on major networks and featured stories on public radio. While many will criticize parents for sharing their children's images in public, society can't get enough of these performances as is evident in the number of contests, requests and rewards that exist to promote and increase the sharing.

There is a great supply and demand for images of children on the web. This chapter merely touches on the types of videos being shared. Entire genres of performances have not even been addressed, such as children preaching, young rappers, school plays, dance pageants and so on. As with the videos discussed in this chapter, others range from private moments made public to public performances being shared in the hopes of getting attention. It is apparent that many users are not aware of the control that they could actually exercise over their privacy, or are aware but are not interested in keeping the performances private. Childhood memories, often saved and shared with only immediate family, are now being broadcast to the world. A recent Hallmark ad says, "Memories are NOT for keeping. They're for giving away." What the Hallmark ad doesn't say is what people are doing with the memories when you give them away. Children's images made public can be co-opted, edited and kept by anyone with access to the content. These individuals can modify context, create false images, alter memories and place both the innocent and the Gremlin child in adult contexts that are sometimes inappropriate. The public nature of these moments of childhood are cause for concern for a child's self-perception and self-determination as they move forward to a future that will almost certainly be even less private than the very public world of today.

Notes

1. Jean Burgess and Joshua Green, *YouTube: Online Video and Participatory Culture* (Cambridge: Polity, 2009), 1–3.

2. "comScore Releases April 2011 U.S. Online Video Rankings," comScore, Inc. www.comscore.com/Press_Events/Press_Releases/2011/5/comScore_Releases_April_20 11_U.S._Online_Video_Rankings (accessed December 6, 2011).

3. YouTube, "Statistics," www.youtube.com/t/press_statistics (accessed December 6, 2011).

4. YouTube, "Thanks, YouTube Community, for Two BIG Gifts on Our Sixth Birthday!"   global.blogspot.com/2011/05/thanks-youtube-community-for-two-big.html (accessed April 29, 2012).

5. Michael Wesch, "An Anthropological Introduction to YouTube," www.youtube.com/watch?v=TPAO-lZ4_hU (accessed April 29, 2012).

6. "YouTube Statistics." Digital Ethnography @ KSU, August 13 2008 ksudigg.wetpaint.com/page/YouTube+Statistics (accessed April 29, 2012).

7. "Star Wars Kid." BBC, news.bbc.co.uk/2/hi/entertainment/6187554.stm (accessed April 29, 2012).

8. YouTube, "Charts," www.youtube.com/charts/videos_views?t=a (accessed April 29, 2012).

9. "Charlie Bit My Finger - Again !" www.youtube.com/watch?v=_OBlgSz8sSM (accessed April 29, 2012).

10. Laipply, Judson, "Evolution of Dance." youtube.com/watch?v=dMH0bHeiRNg.

11. Patricia R. Zimmerman, *Reel Families: A Social History of Amateur Film* (Bloomington: Indiana University Press, 1995), 123.

68   Chapter Four

12. Maria Pini, "Inside the Home Mode," in *Video Cultures: Media Technology and Everyday Creativity*, ed. David Buckingham and Rebecca Willet, 71–29. (Basingstoke, England: Palgrave Macmillan, 2009), 71.

13. James M. Moran, *There's No Place Like Home Video* (Minneapolis: University of Minnesota Press, 2002), 141.

14. Moran, *There's No Place*, 152.

15. Zimmerman, *Reel Families*, 3.

16. Laruen Indvik, "92% of U.S. Toddlers Have Online Presence," Mashable *Social Media*, October 7, 2010, mashable.com/2010/10/07/toddlers-online-presence (accessed April 29, 2012).

17. Bonnie Rochman, "Expected: Child: Facebook Welcomes Fetuses to Social Media," *Healthland Time*, August 3, 2011, healthland.time.com/2011/08/03/expected-child-facebook-welcomes-unborn-babies-to-social-media/#ixzz1fjMdqq1z (accessed April 29, 2012).

18. Indvik, "92%," *Social Media*.

19. Ki Mae Heussner, "Underage Facebook Members: 7.5 Million Users under Age 13," ABC News, May 10 2011, abcnews.go.com/Technology/underage-facebook-members-75-million-users-age-13/story?id=13565619#.Tt6FC0ejJOk (accessed April 29, 2012).

20. "Top 10 YouTube Videos of All Time," ReadWriteweb, August 21 2007. www.readwriteweb.com/archives/top_10_youtube_videos_of_all_time_2007.php (accessed April 29, 2012).

21. Maurice Chittenden, "Harry and Charlie Davies-Carr". *The Sunday Times*, November 1, 2009, www.thesundaytimes.co.uk/sto/ingear/tech_and_net/article189173.ece (accessed April 29, 2012).

22. Mina Hochberg, "YouTube's Child Stars," Babble.com, May 11 2009, www.babble.com/celebrity/celebrity-style/youtube-child-stars-david-at-the-dentist-charlie-bit-me-viral-videos/index3.aspx (accessed April 29, 2012).

23. "Laughing Baby," www.youtube.com/watch?v=HttF5HVYtlQ (accessed April 29, 2012).

24. "David after Dentist." www.youtube.com/watch?v=txqiwrbYGrs (accessed April 29, 2012).

25. Monica Hesse, "'David after Dentist';" *The Washington Post*, April 7, 2010, www.washingtonpost.com/wp-dyn/content/article/2010/04/06/AR2010040603863.html (accessed April 29, 2012).

26. Claire Suddath. "Pop Star 2.0," *Time*, May 17, 2010, 49-50.

27. Hochberg, "YouTube," Babble.com.

28. "More Choice for Users: Unlisted Videos," Broadcasting Ourselves) The Official YouTube Blog. May 12 2010. http://youtube-global.blogspot.com/2010/05/more-choice-for-users-unlisted-videos.html.

29. YouTube, "Children," YouTube Community Guidelines," www.youtube.com/t/community_guidelines (accessed April 29, 2012).

30. YouTube, "YouTube Privacy Notice," www.youtube.com/t/privacy (accessed April 29, 2012).

31. YouTube, "YouTube Terms of Service," www.youtube.com/t/terms (accessed April 29, 2012).

32. Lev Grossman, "Time Person of the Year: You," *Time*, December 25, 2006, 38-41.

33. "YouTube Challenge—I Gave My Kids a Terrible Present," www.youtube.com/watch?v=q4a9CKgLprQ (accessed April 29, 2012).

34. Rebecca Black, "Friday: Official Music Video," youtube.com/watch?v=kfVsfOSbJY0&ob=av3e (accessed April 29, 2012).

35. Todd Wasserman. "How Rebecca Black Became a YouTube Sensation." Mashable, March 16, 2011, mashable.com/2011/03/16/rebecca-black-youtube (accessed April 29, 2012).

36. William Wei, "'The Star Wars Kid' Sued the People Who Made Him Famous." *Business Insider*, May 10 2011, articles.businessinsider.com/2010-05-12/tech/30099127_1_star-wars-kid-viral-video-ghyslain-raza (accessed April 29, 2012).

37. Adrian Chen, "How the Internet Beat Up an 11-Year-Old Girl," *Gawker,* July 16, 2010, gawker.com/5589103/how-the-internet-beat-up-an-11+year+old-girl (accessed April 29, 2012).

38. Frederick Levy, *15 Minutes of Fame: Becoming a Star in the YouTube Revolution* (New York: Penguin Group, 2008).

39. "Emerson—Mommy's Nose Is Scary!" www.youtube.com/watch?v=N9oxmRT2YWw (accessed April 29, 2012).

40. Levy, *15 Minutes.*

41. Brian Stelter, "YouTube Videos Pull In Real Money," *New York Times*, December 10 2008, www.nytimes.com/2008/12/11/business/media/11youtube.html (accessed April 29, 2012).

42. Jonathan Brown, "Revealed: The YouTube Rich List," *Independent*, August 26, 2010, www.independent.co.uk/life-style/gadgets-and-tech/news/revealed-the-youtube-rich-list-2062197.html?action=Gallery&ino=2 (accessed April 29, 2012).

43. "Shaytards. Daily Video Diary," www.youtube.com/user/SHAYTARDS (accessed April 29, 2012).

44. Michael Humphrey, "ShayCarl's Epic Journey to YouTube Stardom," *Forbes.* May 31, 2011, www.forbes.com/sites/michaelhumphrey/2011/05/31/shaycarls-epic-journey-to-youtube-stardom/3/ (accessed April 29, 2012).

45. Monica Hesse, "'David after Dentist' Goes Goliath Online" *The Washington Post*, April 7, 2010. www.washingtonpost.com/wp-dyn/content/article/2010/04/06/AR2010040603863.html.

46. Vanessa Allen, "The Amateur YouTube Stars Making Families £100,000 from Their Hilarious Home Videos," *Daily Mail*, November 14, 2011, www.dailymail.co.uk/news/article-2060939/YouTube-stars-making-families-100-000-hilarious-home-videos.html#ixzz1kxzc4MJ4 (accessed April 29, 2012).

47. Jane Lever, "Letting Charlie Bite the Finger Again," *New York Times*, August 15, 2011, www.nytimes.com/2011/08/15/business/media/letting-charlie-bite-the-finger-again.html (accessed April 29, 2012).

48. Maxwell House, www.brewsomegood.ca/ (accessed April 29, 2012).

49. "YouTube Favorites Jorge and Alexa Narvaez in 2nd Hyundai Commercial Singing 'Home' (Video)," *Hispanically Speaking News*, January 4, 2012, www.hispanicallyspeakingnews.com/notitas-de-noticias/details/youtube-favorites-jorge-and-alexa-narvaez-in-2nd-hyundai-commercial-singing/13096/ (accessed April 29, 2012).

50. Claire Cain Miller, "Cashing in on Your Hit You Tube Video," *New York Times*, October 26, 2011, www.nytimes.com/2011/10/27/technology/personaltech/cashing-in-on-your-hit-youtube-video.html (accessed April 29, 2012).

51. Caroline McCarthy, "Kids on YouTube: How Much Is Too Much?" CNET News, April 14, 2010, news.cnet.com/8301-13577_3-20002416-36.html (accessed April 29, 2012).

52. "Coogan Law," SAG-AFTRA, www.sag.org/content/coogan-law (accessed April 29, 2012).

53. BizParentz Foundation, "Federal Taxes," bizparentz.org/federaltaxes.html (accessed April 29, 2012).

54. McCarthy, "Kids on YouTube," CNET.

55. "David After David After Dentist," *Tosh.0*, January 13, 2010, tosh.comedycentral.com/video-clips/david-after--david-after-dentist- (accessed April 29, 2012).

56. "I Don't Like You Mommy," www.youtube.com/watch?v=E8aprCNnecU (accessed April 29, 2012).

57. Michael Strangelove, *Watching YouTube: Extraordinary Videos by Ordinary People*. (Toronto: University of Toronto Press, 2010).

58. Strangelove, *Watching*, 59.

59. Strangelove, *Watching*, 60.

60. Strangelove, *Watching*, 60.

61. Linda A. Henkel, "Photograph-Induced Memory Errors: When Photographs Make People Claim They Have Done Things They Have Not," *Applied Cognitive Psychology*, 25 (2011): 78–86.

62. Iris Blandon-Gitlin and David Gerkens, "The Effects of Photographs and Event Plausibility in Creating False Beliefs," *Acta Psychologica*, 135 (2010): 330-334.

63. Matt Richtel and Miguel Helft, "Facebook Users Who Are Under Age Raise Concerns," *The New York Times*, March 11, 2011, www.nytimes.com/2011/03/12/technology/internet/12underage.html?_r=1&pagewanted=all (accessed April 29, 2012).

64. Strangelove, *Watching*, 55.

65. "Trevor," www.youtube.com/user/iTr3vor (accessed April 29, 2012).

66. Anne Higonnet, *Pictures of Innocence: The History and Crisis of Ideal Child-*

hood (London: Thames and Hudson Ltd., 1998). 15.

67. Higonnet, *Pictures,* 77.

68. Higonnet, *Pictures,* 86.

69. Gary Cross, *The Cute and the Cool* (London: Oxford University Press, 2004).

70. Cross, *Cute,* 125.

71. Cross, *Cute,* 161.

72. Higonnet, *Pictures,* 225.

73. "My First Hardcore Song by 8 Yr Old Juliet," www.youtube.com/watch?feature=player_embedded&v=uU6U-8LP1DY (accessed April 29, 2012).

74. "My First Hardcore Song Response by 6 Yr Old Jacob www.youtube.com/watch?v=Jeosb5k2yXI (Accessed April 29, 2012).

Chapter Five
Pearly Whites and Spandex Tights: The Imagery of Teeth in *Peter Pan*, Elite Figure Skating and Gymnastics, and Child Beauty Pageants
by Beth Nardella

> Growing up . . . is against the rules.—Barrie, 48.

Teeth, their loss and their gain, go hand-in-hand with all the major milestones of life. The life span of teeth—the associated activities relating to orthodontia, dentist visits, and eventually replacements—is part of the human life cycle from birth to death. Thus, teeth are key signifiers. Teeth reveal class, status, age, commitment to personal hygiene (or lack thereof) and reflect on the kind of parenting one had. In contemporary society white teeth are as cosmetically sought after as silicone implants. In critical theory, they provide a punctum for Barthes (43–44) and are at the very center of Peter Pan's eroticism, at least according to Kincaid (282). In elite gymnastics and figure skating, teeth win the gold. Due to the rising popularity and exposure to child beauty pageants beginning with the death of JonBenet Ramsey in 1996 and increasing with the success of the TLC television reality show *Toddlers and Tiaras*, teeth have again found their way into the spotlight. More recently, teeth gnaw into the debates between the innocence of childhood (childhood lost) and children's agency (childhood found), and the controversy surrounding the politics of child abuse versus the driven child.

Forever Young

All children, except one, grow up. —Barrie, 1

The world of competitive gymnastics and figure skating acutely parallels
that of Peter Pan and his Neverland. Young girls (Wendys) are forced to grow
up fast and act like adults, something which Peter refuses to do. They often train
eight to ten hours a day, longer than the average person's workday. Just as
Wendy flew across the sea to become a mother to the Lost Boys and her Peter,
darning socks, cooking meals, making pockets ("None of us has any pockets").
and enforcing bedtime, many athletes move away from home and family to live
with coaches. Perhaps the saddest similarity lies within the athletes. While being
forced to grow up emotionally, they are also forced to stay young, little and with
girl-child bodies—a mixture of both Peter and Wendy.

Karen Reid, a gymnast who developed obsessive compulsive disorder
because of the intense rituals of competition and training said: "There is always
the pressure to look so young too. You always wanted to look like a little girl. It
was like a sin to grow up" (Ryan 138–9). Viewers and judges want a small
body. This trend makes winners out of twelve- and thirteen-year-old girls whose
bodies have yet to show a hint of puberty. Imagine Peter Pan with the beard he
so fears. He would never have the charisma we desire. "I don't want to ever be a
man . . . I want always to be a little boy and to have fun" (26). In fact, he isn't
even sure of his own age—he can only assert that he is "quite young." In his
book *Child-Loving: The Erotic Child and Victorian Culture*, James Kincaid
writes, "Peter sees adulthood as a trap and is willing to give up everything in
order not to fall into it" (278). For Kincaid, Peter has a choice. It is his decision
to remain a child. He stubbornly refuses to stay with the Darlings and be
adopted along with the other Lost Boys. Peter is terrified of adulthood.
Jacqueline Rose, however, sees that "Peter Pan is a little boy who does not grow
up, not because he doesn't want to, but because someone else prefers that he
shouldn't" (3). Rose strips away Peter's agency and places the onus on Barrie
and the reader. The reader sees his/her childhood in Peter and desires for him to
remain forever a boy. This speaks to the longing and nostalgia for the reader's
lost childhood.

Critics of competitive sports (be it gymnastics or beauty pageants) for the
very young child cite the role of fanatical parents. These parents are
characterized as pressuring their children into the elite levels of activities to
overcompensate for their own failings, our own desires. Joan Ryan's *Little Girls
in Pretty Boxes* discusses more than one case of hyper-parenting in which
parents or coaches force children to practice long hours after injury, compete
with broken bones, or perform a routine until it's flawless (27). Less discussed
than the driven parent is the driven child—a driven child like Peter Pan. Peter's
obstinacy is a key character trait. Despite his desire for a mother, he refuses the

offer when given. It is quite clear that he knows what he wants. Many elite athletes are the same.

In her 2008 memoir, *Chalked Up*, 1986 U.S.A. National Gymnastics champion Jennifer Sey explains that she was an extremely driven, competitive child. She makes it apparent that had they tried, her parents could not have prevented her from trying to reach her goal of becoming a winner. However, they clearly supported her decision by paying for the extra training, coaching, and travel. While she doesn't condone harsh treatment from coaches toward athletes, she discusses that even as a child she understood that, "this is what it takes to raise a champion." In an interview after the publication of her book she explained, "I signed up to be a champion and I put myself in their hands and they gave that to me. So I don't think they would view any of their practices or tactics as outside the norm because they gave me what I asked for" (NPR). While describing how she was the one who begged to change gyms and go to more practices, she insists that she blames no one but herself. Nevertheless, she strongly defends young girls who experienced callous training methods and poor treatment at the hands of coaches. She believes that, "participating in any sport at the very highest level probably involves these types of practices. I think that the situation is exacerbated in gymnastics because the girls are so young and probably not likely to stand up for themselves and say, 'you know what, I'm not okay with being treated this way'" (NPR). At the heart of this issue is a vast contradiction: the driven child who takes responsibility and the child who is too little to make the right choices for him/herself. These two children are the same being. The life of a competitive athlete (or musician or dancer or singer) is full of rigorous training and people who don't necessarily have the child's best (healthiest) interests in mind. While Sey continually claims that *Chalked Up* is her story, a coming-of-age story, based on her unique and personal experiences, the truth is that this story is not uncommon. These children are being forced (or forcing themselves) to grow up too fast.

Unfortunately, sports such as gymnastics and figure skating demand girl bodies. Even though the scoring has been recently changed to avoid as much bias as possible, it is clear that the more graceful skaters and the perkiest gymnasts are the ones who score higher. Smaller bodies can jump higher and flip faster. While the sports require adultlike poise and grace and an ability to withstand great amounts of pressure—all while looking good—it is impossible to succeed in them as grown women. Written into an understanding of these sports is this unattainable dichotomy. It is the same for Wendy—despite her still being a child while in Neverland, she mentally and emotionally takes on the role of mother for Peter, the Lost Boys, and her brothers. In the end, "she grew up of her own free will a day quicker than other girls" (Barrie, 162). The experience only cost her one day of childhood. When Peter returns to Wendy's room long after she's grown up and become a mother herself, he doesn't recognize her or understand what has happened. He accepts her daughter Jane as a replacement and takes her to an unchanged Neverland. "Of course," writes Barrie, "in the end Wendy let them fly away together" (168).

Seen through the lens of feminist criticism one must wonder of Jane: did she exercise choice? At the same time the act of allowing Jane to go to Neverland gives readers (and Wendy) the imagined possibility that Jane will forever remain that perfect child. Perhaps these are the decisions parents of elite athletes struggle with: do they support their children regardless of their own reservations (provided they have them) or do they lock the window?

The Children are Carried Off

Oh, why can't you remain like this for ever!—Barrie, 1

As their perfect preadolescent bodies score them points on the ice and in the ring, it's their smiles that bring in the gold. In 1993, when Nancy Kerrigan was twenty-three, *People* magazine selected her as one of its "50 Most Beautiful People." After being persuaded by her coaches to get her teeth capped, she went from being America's blue-collar skater to the Ice Princess (Ryan 128). Since Chaucer wrote of the Wife of Bath in the fourteenth century, having a gap between your teeth has indicated sensuality. In her essay, "The Teeth of Desire," Janne Goldbeck explains that this "translated into a desire for fullness of life, and 'womanliness,' though it was not associated with indiscriminate sexuality" (31). Growing up Goldbeck was told that it was a positive trait to have a gap because it was something different from everyone else. Kerrigan's imperfect teeth set her apart in a way that wasn't favorable to the judges or sponsors. After having her teeth fixed she only won the bronze medal at the 1992 Olympics, yet her endorsements increased to the point where she was making as much as gold-medalist Kristi Yamaguchi (Ryan 128). Ironically, the new teeth made Kerrigan appear older and more mature while her former smile had enhanced her girlish quality. At a time when she was beginning to age out of the sport, newer, younger girls were taking titles. But perfecting her smile further removed her from her blue-collar roots, playing into a character wearing costumes designed by Vera Wang, and helping her embody youthfulness in her routines.

Peter's baby teeth are integral to his character. It's his milk teeth, his first "little pearls" that fascinate Mrs. Darling and the reader. Whether "clad in skeleton leaves and the juices that ooze out of trees" (Barrie, 10) or layered in Hook's flashy pirate clothes, the very essence of Peter is his perfect baby teeth which are markers that he is barely out of toddlerhood. Barrie writes that Mrs. Darling "was melted because he had all his first teeth" (92). Historically, in the United States and elsewhere, the loss of the first tooth is seen as more than just an indication of physical development. Jennifer Eastman Attebery writes in "From Tooth Fairy to Long in the Tooth: Reflection on Anglo-American Tooth-lore" that teeth are "a sign of more than just physical—but also intellectual—maturity" (61). She lists several examples from folklore and popular culture.

The first, gleaned from elementary school teachers, is that losing the first tooth signals a readiness to learn how to read. Solid arguments, she explains, "have teeth," while poor reasoning is "toothless." Attebery sees teeth as "the seat of the mature mental powers of rumination and discernment" (61). As well, Peter uses his teeth to great advantage. He is certainly the ruler of Neverland—all the residents there look up to him as such. He also appears to be the youngest. If he still has his baby teeth, he can be no older than five or six years old. Yet he is so charismatic as to have everyone (especially Hook) under his spell. Although the phrase "a colt's tooth" is often used to refer to an older person who desires someone or something much younger than himself, it suits Peter perfectly. With his spirited ways and reckless abandon, he lives free and simply, passionately and with the delight of a child, while possessing the wisdom gained from his lived experiences (that he so often claims to forget). Goldbeck writes, "To have colt's teeth in a mature head is perverse, but to maintain one's zest for life and openness to experience at any age doesn't seem so reprehensible" (33). How fitting. What is it about teeth—and losing them, gnashing them, and flashing them—that they have held everyone's interest for so long?

Barthes tells us that the erotic is fleeting, fragmented, flirtatious. Is Peter anything but? Part of Peter's eroticism is that he only flashes us his teeth, and the rest is his attitude. For Hook, it is this attitude that is so maddening. Barrie writes:

> The truth is that there was a something about Peter which goaded the pirate captain to frenzy. It was not his courage, it was not his engaging appearance, it was . . . Peter's cockiness. This had got on Hook's nerves. It made his iron claw twitch, and at night it disturbed him like an insect." (115–116)

Peter has everything Hook does not; Hook ages, Peter gloats. He is at the age where most children have an increased awareness that they are growing up and what this means: that they (all except one) won't stay the same forever. Barrie mentions this on the first page of the novel: "You always know after you are two. Two is the beginning of the end" (1). This is when children finally have all their first teeth and have yet to lose them. They have the ability to articulate their wants and needs and rarely hesitate to do so. But Peter has chosen not to grow up and relishes his difference. Hook hates this and sets out to kill him. However, when he finds Peter, seeming smug to Hook even while asleep, he is unable to act.

This is what "steeled Hook's heart" as he spies Peter sleeping: "One arm dropped over the edge of the bed, one leg was arched, and the unfinished part of his laugh was stranded on his mouth, which was open, showing the little pearls. . . . The open mouth, the drooping arm, the arched knee: they were such a personification of cockiness as, taken together, will never again one may hope to be presented to eyes so sensitive to their offensiveness" (Barrie, 121–122). Hook had his chance to finally end his arch nemesis and passed it up. He was too taken by our boy hero. Although he's full of rage, he doesn't act; he doesn't even wake Peter up. Hook, instead, poisons the boy's drink, leaving his death up to chance. He then brags about what he's done, muttering to himself through the Neverland forest. Tinker Bell overhears the bragging and rescues Peter by drinking the poison herself. Hook's fascination with Peter and his own arrogance are what lead to Peter being saved. Kincaid writes that Hook "is obsessed with Peter, cannot leave off looking for and at him" (285). He is single-minded. After he believes he has killed Peter, instead of joy, Hook feels loneliness. "Hook," writes Barrie, "was profoundly dejected" (129). When your desires have been fulfilled, you have nothing left to long for—such is their fleeting nature.

Gender and Beyond Gender

And they were ours, ours, and now they are gone.—Barrie, 15

Kincaid states that Peter is beyond gender. In the theater the role is traditionally played by adult females who have the experience to present a solid performance but the build of a boy. In the 1904 play, *Peter Pan*, on which the popular novel was based, the character of Peter was played by a woman. Subsequent productions have continued with the tradition of featuring women in the lead including the Broadway musical starring Mary Martin, and more recently gymnast Cathy Rigby (Hanson 173, 259). As written, Peter seems to be trying out a role, toying with gender. While he pretends to be tough and certainly follows through with action, he is fragile. This is all an act. Peter performs childhood. This is why he is so appealing. He is an old soul with the body of a boy. Kincaid explains why we are drawn to him: "His erotic fascination [is] focused especially in his pearly teeth. His most provocative acts come when he sends energy into these teeth . . . energy about to explode" (282, 285).

It is the same for the elite athletes. Because their bodies have yet to reach puberty, these young girls *perform* femininity, they perform adulthood. Ice skaters wear costumes with faux (flesh-toned) plunging necklines and short skirts. They have strict rules set by the International Skating Union and they work within and around those parameters. Their costumes give the illusion of nudity while remaining concealing. Gymnasts wear a lot of makeup and they embellish their routines with elaborate gestures and broad smiles, flashing those glistening teeth. They have less freedom in costume and hair design than figure skaters due to the team nature of the sport (accessories would hinder movement).

Pageant attire is by far the most outrageous. Unlike the Shirley Temple dresses and bobby socks of earlier pageants, today's girls are dressed in evening wear that could rival that worn by Miss America contestants (ages seventeen through twenty-four). For talent portions of the competitions, girls have been known to dress like Las Vegas showgirls, a "Vogue" era Madonna, and Dallas Cowboy cheerleaders. The similarities to drag are overwhelming. Like the gay men who perform as Cher or Liza Minnelli, these girls are performing womanhood with impeccably groomed eyebrows, hair extensions, and padded bras. They play a caricature of an adult woman who doesn't actually exist.

In spite of these efforts of the athletes and pageant girls to look older, they are fixed as little girls with the same fears as Peter of growing up. Growing up signifies much for these girls: a loss of ability and aging out of the sport; being less attractive to judges; and leaving the spotlight. Perhaps it is because of this that many athletes go on to be coaches and judges after they retire from the sport, perpetuating the same conditions under which they competed.

Peter clearly fears growing up (manhood, having a beard) but he also seems to fear mothers and women. His nightmares expose these fears: "Sometimes, though not often," writes Barrie, "he had dreams, and they were more painful than the dreams of other boys. For hours he could not be separated from these dreams, though he wailed piteously in them. They had to do, I think, with the riddle of his existence" (121). Like the young female athletes, the nature of growing up is intricately complex and an arduous task.

Young athletes battle eating disorders and suffer from severe injuries. The emotional toll can last long into adulthood. Clinical psychologist Mary Pipher and media/communications theorist Neil Postman would argue that all childhoods, not just those of elite athletes, are already lost. Contemporary society, rampant with the negative influence of the mainstream media, has taken it all away. Children already know everything; they are forced to grow up too fast. It is the opposite of Peter's remaining a boy forever. Today's children, according to Pipher and Postman, don't get to be children at all.

In *The Disappearance of Childhood*, Neil Postman writes that childhood was invented with movable type. He feels that increased literacy throughout the population created "adult secrets" and with them, children who did not have access to those secrets. Thus children were separate from adults, unlike in medieval times where children were just smaller people, wearing the same styles of clothing, eating the same foods, doing the same types of labor, and engaging in the same leisure activities. With literacy came education. Education, he writes, beget the idea that children were no longer ungrown adults but "unformed adults" (41). He then blames television for the disappearance of childhood. He claims that through television, an equal-opportunity destroyer, children learned the "adult secrets" and therefore their innocence was lost. Further he claims that the Women's Liberation Movement, from Second-Wave Feminism, led women into the workplace and away from the home, leaving children neglected and less nurtured (151). He concludes that eventually, society will return to the barbarous and uncivilized state of the Middle Ages, where there are once again no demarcations between children and adults as evidenced by the use of foul language, provocative children's clothing, and organized sports (129). What Postman fails to do is explain why these things are hurting our children, although his tone clearly implies these activities are fatal to an outdated definition of childhood. Imagine if Postman, who died in 2003, had seen the current state of the Internet. Many will agree that it's shocking to hear a little kid shouting profanities or dancing provocatively in the talent portion of a beauty pageant. Why does this behavior provoke such a response? It can be argued that children, while cognizant of the "adultness" of this conduct, still aren't aware of the full sexual *meaning* of it.

In the 1990s, Pipher's bestseller *Reviving Ophelia* appeared to be an important book for the decade. She discusses in graphic detail the issues that contemporary girls face and the pressures they have to fit into society's molds. Pipher begins by explaining how little she understood about today's teenager before she began writing, how much times had changed in the thirty years since she had been a teenager, and the day-to-day roller coaster she felt her daughter was riding just being in adolescence. As a therapist, she was working with girls in crisis: eating disorders, suicide attempts, rape, drug abuse, venereal disease, cutting, divorced parents, pregnancy, and anything terrible you can imagine. She juxtaposes these tragic stories against idyllic stories of her own childhood set in a small Midwestern town. While the book is not meant to be sensationalist, it reads as such. She paints a vividly terrifying picture for any mother of a girl. Pipher illustrates that "the parents' job is to protect" while their daughters explore (23). After reading her book, no parent would let his or her children out of the house (not forgetting to throw out the television and burn all the fashion magazines). Referring to the African saying, "It takes a village to raise a child," Pipher laments that "the protected place in space and time that we once called childhood has grown shorter. Most girls no longer have a village" (28) and, Pipher claims further that childhood is much more difficult than it ever was. Aside from anecdotes on violent crimes, she offers little evidence to why. How are today's challenges different than those of thirty years ago or even 100 years ago? She seems to suggest, like Postman, the only distinction is that we have increased media reporting these negative events.

Pipher also discusses how girls today are being sent mixed signals (35), that they are in "rigorous training for the female role" (39), learning that to succeed in life they must pretend to be something they are not. "Girls are trained to be less than who they really are. They are trained to be what the culture wants of its young women, not what they themselves want to become" (44). Again, she provides little evidence of this beyond what she has gleaned from her patients. While few middle- and high-school students will disagree with Pipher that being a teenager can be a challenging, horrible time in life, and few adults who have survived it would agree to relive it if given the chance, certainly not all girls are having this tough a go of it. Like Postman, she presents a gloom-and-doom story based on personal experience and observations without offering an acceptable solution for girls or their parents or positing that dystopia is not the norm.

Lauren Berlant takes a different approach to a similar problem by deconstructing Tipper Gore's *Raising PG Kids in an X-Rated Society*. In *The Queen of America Goes to Washington City* she presents many of the same issues facing girls today but in the larger framework of the American citizen.

Instead of blaming television and the media for society's woes, she analyzes some of the tactics used by those entities to set a proper point of view for a postmodern society. Berlant "adjusts the perspective on the innocent, pre-historical infantile citizen by looking at a horror currently organized around her body" (21). Her main argument focuses on how extremist groups have "intensified the image of the ideal citizen as an innocent young girl or the young girl's parent" (22). In challenging the idea of the model American that Gore establishes, Berlant implies that parents shouldn't need a label to make proper decisions. She explains that Gore conflates the image of the parent with that of an infant, a vulnerable minor unable to make informed decisions against the barrage of explicit media sales tactics. Berlant places Gore in the camp with Postman and Pipher, who blame the loss of innocent childhoods on the decline of the family and the pressure of the media.

The media is being held responsible for countless atrocities against our children. Parents are being held responsible for letting their children be exposed to the media. While certainly many children have been harmed by the careless and even deliberate actions of others, would it be so wrong to assume that most of us are doing just fine? Perhaps most of us are, for the most part, like Peter, generally carefree, with just an occasional bad dream.

Social Class

There was always the possibility that the next time you fell he would let you go.—
Barrie, 37

The media is also faulted for its representations of social class. Television shows tend to portray stereotypes in order to appeal to a wider audience. However, photography can depict social class on levels that other mediums cannot. In William Klein's photograph *Little Italy. New York, 1954*, Barthes finds a punctum in the lack of glistening whiteness in the boy's smile. "What I stubbornly see," he writes, "are one child's bad teeth" (45). What Barthes doesn't consider is that maybe the kid in the photo can't afford braces. Maybe his parents are waiting for him to grow up (unlike Barthes) and let the new teeth push out his rotten "little pearls." It's also possible that neither he nor his parents actually care.

In America, teeth are a sign of social class. Stereotypes of the working class often include images of bad teeth, while the wealthy can afford whitening treatments and cosmetic dentistry. Pageant moms often force their children to wear "flippers"—plastic covers for teeth—that cover up missing baby teeth and enhance a smile. Similarly, figure skaters often have dental work done to make their teeth stand out to the judges. But it goes deeper than that. If you have good teeth, you have a good mother—not just a good enough mother. The mothers of these young gymnasts and figure skaters, and the pageant girls too, are preparing their children to grow up while trying to keep them in their small bodies. These bodies become empty vessels onto which viewers project their own ideas of childhood.

Just like in gymnastics, it takes a certain kind of child—a driven child— someone who wants to be a winner, a pleaser, to rise to the elite levels of any activity. Studies have shown that girls who competed in beauty pageants as children are more likely to have eating disorders. There are countless stories of gymnasts and figure skaters who have both fallen victim to and conquered anorexia and bulimia (Cathy Rigby, who played Peter Pan on Broadway, is one example). Wonderlich, Ackard, and Henderson consider the effect of beauty pageants on mental health in their 2005 study. They write, "A variety of biological, psychological, and environmental risk factors have been linked to disordered eating behavior and negative body image" (291). Society promotes beauty standards of perfection and thinness. The researchers specifically investigated the levels of depression, body dissatisfaction, and lower self-esteem in adulthood as a result of participation in childhood beauty pageants. Not surprisingly, they found that feelings of ineffectiveness were increased in subjects who had participated in the pageants. In addition, they demonstrated higher levels of interpersonal distrust, body dissatisfaction, and faulty impulse control (296). Wonderlich, Ackard and Henderson do, however, comment on the possibility that women who compete in beauty pageants may have personality types predisposed to disordered eating (299). Indeed, research has consistently shown that there is a "type" of female more prone to be affected by eating disorders (Anderluh and Westen). Perhaps future research could examine the correlation between personality type and elite athletes/competitors.

Of course, little progress can be made in any elite circuit without parental involvement. Overzealous or not, someone must pay for the practices and the equipment or costumes, someone must drive the children to the activities, and someone must encourage the children to continue. This raises the question of who is to blame? Is it child abuse for parents to facilitate their children's desires or are ambitious children driving themselves toward eating disorders and burnout? Is childhood lost or was it already gone before we got there? For many reasons, teeth are at the center of these debates. From the first milk teeth through flippers and beyond, teeth signify a coming of age and a gaining of wisdom. Peter Pan's teeth are signifiers of the eternal child; many children find childhood cut extremely short by choosing (or being chosen) to grow up. Kincaid feels that we think of children as "fillable with whatever we have to have." Our desires to make them what we want them to be (what we once or never were) cause them to grow up terribly fast, with the "speed of darkness."

Works Cited

Anderluh, Marija Brecelj, Kate Tchanturia, Sophia Rabe-Hesketh, and Janet Treasure. "Childhood Obsessive-Compulsive Personality Traits in Adult Women with Eating Disorders: Defining a Broader Eating Disorder Phenotype." *American Journal of Psychiatry.* 160 (2003): 242–247.

Attebery, Jennifer Eastman. "From Tooth Fairy to Long in the Tooth: Reflection on Anglo-American Tooth-Lore." *Rendezvous Journal.* 37 (2002–2003): 59–62.

Barrie, J.M. *Peter Pan.* New York: Bantam Books, 1985.

Barthes, Roland. *Camera Lucida.* Translated by Richard Howard. New York: Hill and Wang, 1981.

Berlant, Lauren. *The Queen of America Goes to Washington City: Essays on Sex and Citizenship.* Durham, NC: Duke University Press, 1997.

Goldbeck, Janne. "The Teeth of Desire." *Rendezvous Journal.* 37 (2002-2003): 31-33.

Hanson, Bruce K. *The Peter Pan Chronicles: The Nearly 100 Year History of the Boy That Wouldn't Grow Up.* New York: Birch Lane Press, 1993.

Kincaid, James. *Child-Loving: The Erotic Child and Victorian Culture.* New York: Routledge, 1992.

National Public Radio. "Elite Gymnastics Not All It's Chalked Up to Be." *Talk of the Nation.* 1 May 2008. http://www.npr.org/templates/story/story.php? storyId= 90105904 (accessed 11 July 11, 2011).

People Magazine. "Fifty Most Beautiful People: Nancy Kerrigan." *People.* 3 May 1993. Vol. 39, No. 17. http://www.people.com/people/archive/article/0,,20110331,00.html. (accessed 14 April 2012).

Pipher, Mary. *Reviving Ophelia: Saving the Selves of Adolescent Girls.* New York: Ballantine Books, 1994.

Postman, Neil. *The Disappearance of Childhood.* New York: Delacorte Press, 1982.

Rose, Jacqueline. *The Case of Peter Pan, or the Impossibility of Children's Fiction.* Philadelphia: University of Pennsylvania Press, 1993.

Ryan, Joan. *Little Girls in Pretty Boxes: The Making and Breaking of Elite Gymnasts and Figure Skaters.* New York: Warner Books, 2000.

Sey, Jennifer. *Chalked Up: Inside Elite Gymnastics' Merciless Coaching, Overzealous Parents, Eating Disorders, and Elusive Olympic Dreams.* New York: William Morrow, 2008.

Westen, Drew and Jennifer Harnden-Fischer. "Personality Profiles in Eating Disorders: Rethinking the Distinction Between Axis I and Axis II." *American Journal of Psychiatry* (2001): 547– 562.

Wonderlich, Anna L., Diann M. Ackard and Judith B. Henderson. "Childhood Beauty Pageant Contestants: Associations with Adult Disordered Eating and Mental Health." *Eating Disorders.* 13 (2005): 291–301.

Chapter Six
Conceptualizing Childhood in the Korean Educational Broadcasting System (EBS): A Critical Analysis of Pororo
by Lena Lee

Introduction

Children of many countries first encounter formalized socialization through early childhood education (ECE). This socialization includes complex social values, interests, and concerns. A critical analysis of early childhood education in a specific society provides an understanding of societal and cultural beliefs that are deemed important enough to introduce to young citizens. Identifying hidden assumptions and myths in the field of early childhood education raises questions about the beliefs and practices that have been dominant and taken for granted in the educational structures and institutions of a specific society (James, Jenks, and Prout 1998). Therefore, to look closely at everyday educational practices and discourse can be a useful way to understand education and schools as a part of social reality (Popkewitz 1986).

However, young children's learning does not occur only in schools. Media and popular culture are vehicles for teaching particular social roles, values, and ideals to children. These sites may be even more influential than traditionally formalized institutions such as family, church, and public schools (Giroux 1995). Popular culture contains venues by which children have direct and unmediated access to information, knowledge, and culture; as such they may be regarded as more intimately meaningful to them than official school knowledge (e.g., Corsaro 2003; Giroux 1995).

Currently, young children have unprecedented access to popular culture. Adult concerns regarding the powerful influence of television on children, particularly young children, which surfaced early in the medium's history spurred the creation of educational programming. In Belgium, England, Germany, Japan, Korea, the Netherlands, and the United States, for instance, the educational broadcasting networks continue to develop programs, with the input of ECE professionals, to educate children who have been born and who live in a techno-media era (Fisch 2004; Lemish 2007; Wright et al. 2001). One could argue, then, that contemporary early childhood education practices and discourses are pursued outside of schools via television on an international scale. From this perspective, an early childhood program of the educational broadcasting network is closely intertwined with social values and its expectations like other educational mechanisms in society. Considering the close relationships between the educational broadcasting programs and society, this chapter discusses the Korean educational broadcasting network in order to examine what values and expectations are embedded. It will focus on the ways in which the Korean network portrays the concepts of "childhood" and "children." This chapter particularly examines how young children and early childhood are defined in a Korean popular picture book series, *Pororo*. This series is based on an educational TV program for young children developed by the Korean educational broadcasting network, Educational Broadcasting System (EBS). In situating the analysis of the concepts which underlie the series, this chapter begins to discuss prevailing conceptions of childhood socially, particularly with regard to "innocence" and "ignorance."

Notions of Childhood and Media

Innocent Childhood

In many Western societies the view of children as dependent on adults is a part of developmental theories in which children are seen as helpless and presocial (Archard 1993; Cannella 1997; Christian-Smith and Erdman 1997; James, Jenks, and Prout 1998; James and Prout 1997; Jenks 1982; Walkerdine 1984). Moreover, such a perspective is contained in the notion of innocence, as well as the notions of vulnerability and ignorance commonly associated with young children. Therefore, it is believed that young children's lives should be regulated and protected in order to make childhood "a careful, safe, secure and happy phase of human existence" (James and Prout 1997, 191).

The notion of innocence is derived in part from both Western Christian images and the Rousseauian idea of childhood by formulating a dichotomy of childhood and adulthood. As Archard (1993) stated, "Children are seen as nearest to God, whilst adults, correlatively, are furthest from Him" (37). In other words, children are seen as having a pure nature, which comes from their recent arrival in the world, but society will corrupt that purity. This image of childhood is opposed to another concept of childhood, one that sees a child as being born in original sin. The doctrine of original sin was a critical belief of the Puritans from the seventeenth to the early nineteenth century in Western societies, and the Puritans sought to break a child's will, since they believed that children were bad as a result of a lack of both wisdom and knowledge (Cleverly and Phillips 1976; Greven 1988). Thus, "most modern strategies of child protection are underpinned by theories of pollution" in which adult society is thought to "undermine childhood innocence," implying that children must be segregated from "the harsh realities of the adult world and protected from social danger" (James and Prout 1997, 191). This perspective of the need to protect children implies that adults or social organizations such as schools must control and monitor children, because this world is too decadent, hazardous, and precarious for innocent, vulnerable, and ignorant children.

The Disruptive Influence of Media

Several scholars (Elkind 1981 & 1998; Kline 1993; Postman 1994; Steinberg and Kincheloe 1997) have yet suggested that such a conception of childhood is problematic. One of the important reasons for regarding this notion of childhood as problematic was that children have been exposed to an overwhelming amount of information through the mass media and many other technologies. According to these critics, media and technologies have destroyed childhood innocence by compounding childhood with adulthood. Moreover, children are seen as passive audiences as well as consumers in media culture:

There is a sense in which pictures and other graphic images may be said to be "cognitively repressive." Television has the potential to put our minds to sleep. People watch television. They do not read it. Nor do they much listen to it. Television offers a fairly primitive but irresistible alternative to the linear and sequential logic of the printed word and tends to make the rigors of a literate education irrelevant. Watching television not only requires no skills but develops no skills . . . it does not make complex demands on either mind or behaviour. (Postman 1983, 78–80)

Concerns about children's exposure to mass media, which results from "the notion of childhood innocence and ignorance and, by extension, adult wisdom and enlightenment" (Kenway and Bullen 2001, 78), is also found in the discourse of children's popular culture. Adults in many societies tend to accuse the media culture of making children depraved and self-indulgent :

Adults are concerned about children's individualistic and maverick styles of behavior. Such matters are of consequence for teachers who are no longer the source of authoritative knowledge and who also have to deal with what they see as children's bad manners, impudence, bravado and egotism. (Kenway and Bullen 2001, 78)

Because of this recent and significant change of childhood from the past, many societies have had adult concerns and tension about the "ungovernability" (78) of children. Adults in general would be deprived of their "control over the knowledge and experiences that are available to children." (Bazalgette and Buckingham 1995). From this point of view, adults regard children as not only being "in danger" from the consumer culture, but also as being "dangerous to the adult order" because of their access to adult knowledge through that culture (Kenway and Bullen 2001, 79).

Socially Constructed Childhood

The aforementioned perspectives of childhood reflect the expectation of a good childhood, which is "not one in which the essence is freedom and happiness; rather it is good behavior, a deference to adults, and a commitment to learning skills essential for the adult world" (Cunningham 1995, 180). As a matter of fact, statements about children's needs convey an element of judgment about what is good for them and how this can be achieved (e.g., Dearden 1968; Hood-Williams 2001; Schaffer 1990; Stainton-Rogers 1989; Woodhead 1997). Statements such as "X needs Y" generally imply a hypothesis about the goal that results from meeting the need as well as the consequences of failing to do so, since the statement "X needs Y" is apparently an abbreviation of "X needs Y, for Z to follow." According to Woodhead's (1997) argument, Z can be a desirable goal for X, and Y is a way to achieve, or is a precondition for Z. The discourse of "needs" therefore implies "empirical and evaluative claims," which depend on a consensus of knowledge and values in society (Woodhead 1997, 66).

According to the points of view above, children's needs are not merely part of the description of the psychological nature of children. They are also viewed as the basis for specific childhood experiences that are most valued and most frequently adopted in society. Children's needs are a matter of cultural interpretation, which must be context-specific and may well vary in a given context depending on the social values and beliefs (Hood-Williams 2001; Schaffer 1990). In other words: "a statement about children's needs would depend on value, judgments, stated or implied, about which patterns of early relationship are considered desirable, what the child should grow up to become, and indeed what makes for the 'good society'" (Woodhead 1997, 73). In this regard, it is not the children, but adults and society as a whole who determine what a child's needs are in education and with regard to their future. The concept of children's needs based on developmental theories can become "a powerful rhetorical device" in forming images of young childhood and care and the education of children (Woodhead 1997, 77).

Discussions about media and popular culture reflect hidden social assumptions, values, and expectations of children. These implicit social ideologies also determine what knowledge in the media and popular culture is considered desirable for or inappropriate to young children. In associating social values with children's media, it is important to note that different social realities play a crucial role in determining them. Each socio-cultural situation significantly contributes not only to mold the construction of childhood, but also to provide the reasons why a given society conceives of specific children's needs by means of the media. As a result, a program for young children on the Korean educational broadcasting system is likely to represent these social agenda by using media as an instructional tool. By looking closely at what social expectations counted for and how they were practiced in a program of the Korean educational broadcasting network, this chapter intends to understand how the Korean educational media embedded specific social ideologies to construct the images of young children and early childhood.

Pororo: A Korean Educational Animation Series for Young Children

In 1981, the Korean governmental television system (KBS) established an educational broadcasting system (EBS) aiming at enhancing education related not only to the public education system, but also for general audiences, including adult citizens. The EBS became independent in 1990 and is now governed by the Korean Educational Development Institute (KEDI). Before the EBS, a government-operated TV channel (Korean Broadcasting System) provided educational programs such as elementary curriculum related programs begun in 1956 and supplemental and advanced curriculum program for elementary to secondary education begun in 1963.

The EBS created several programs to develop young children's imaginations and creativity. As remarked before, many societies have a skeptical view about popular culture; it can be viewed as a threat to high culture and as a way of destroying childhood innocence (e.g., Elkind 1981 & 1998; Postman 1994). The media and popular culture are thus seen to lead to confusion in the existing social order. Korean adults have also worried about children's exposure to the negative impact of the mass media, which could lead to children's alienation from social relationships, an increase in violent behaviors, and moral decay. Many programs of the EBS well considered this social concern about media. By attempting to exploit on the concept of "edutainment" in the media (e.g., Buckingham and Scanlon 2002), the programs contain carefully selected components of entertainment as well as education to meet both children's interests in and adults' apprehension about the media and popular culture. The edutainment programs intend to promote children's learning processes with combination of the contents of learning and those of play by attracting and maintaining their attention through media (Buckingham and Scanlon 2002; Egenfeldt-Nielsen 2007; Green and McNeese 2007). Such efforts of edutainment, therefore, serve an impulse to "bridge the polarity between schools (education) and recreation (play) that dominate modern childhood" (Ito 2006, 140).

One of the most successful EBS animated programs for young children is *Pororo*. The series focuses on Pororo, a young, curious penguin and his different animal friends. Aimed at young children—mostly preschoolers (three-to-five-year-olds), it has been developed by three different companies, Ocon, SKBoard Band, and EBS. Since its 2003 debut, its popularity has continued to increase. After gaining $150,000 in royalties during the first year, its annual royalty has reached $1.2 to $1.5 million in 2011. This popularity extends outside of Korea. The show appears in more than 110 different countries including Singapore, Indonesia, Hong Kong, France, Italy, Denmark, and Spain (Cha 2011). The characters of the *Pororo* are used in various cultural products: they are licensed approximately to 130 different companies which produced over 1,500 items including books, toys, dolls, school supplies, merchandising, fashion, and food (Cha 2011).

Pororo's success is due to a number of factors (Cha 2011; Jung 2009). First, it resulted from its characters. Many young children tend to be attracted to the unique selection of animals that they do not often see around them. The bisectional body shapes used to illustrate these characters also allow young children to identify more easily with a body structure similar to that of young children.

Second, the *Pororo* has story plots that are developmentally appropriate and interesting to young children (e.g., Cha 2011; Jung 2009; Jung, Jung, and Lee 2010). The story lines center on the everyday life the principals. In the stories, moreover, all of the characters are friends with one another. There is no adult authority figure such as a parent and a teacher in this series. In this way, the *Pororo* focuses on how to lead young children to develop empathy, which is a basic concept for interacting with others (Damon 1988), rather than obeying authority.

Methodology

As mentioned above, this chapter examines the *Pororo* particularly by scrutinizing its representations of being a "good" child. It looks closely at how such representations are interconnected with Korean socio-cultural values and beliefs about children and early childhood.

In this study, nine Pororo picture books were purposefully chosen based on their content: *Pororo and the Magic Flute*; *It Is Time for Potty*; *It Is Time for Getting Up*; *I Can Do, Too*; *Hello, Friend, Crong*; *Red Hat, Patty*; *I Want to Fly*; *Be Careful, Crong!*; *Pororo and the Robot Cook*.

The data were analyzed by latent content analysis which involved interpretation of implicit meanings underlying what is said or shown. The underlying meaning of a text was extracted by repeated readings; an overall assessment was made of the degree to which the work's meanings were described (Fraenkel and Wallen 2000). Several possible themes were constructed from the data analysis; these were revised as deemed necessary. As more information about these themes was collected, it was used to establish more appropriate and detailed subcategories.

Facial expressions of the characters and the background images were examined. The findings from these investigations were then compared to the themes gathered from the latent content analysis described above. In particular, the data in this chapter were closely examined based on how the concepts of helping others and self-regulation were described in the *Pororo* as important characteristics for a child to have in order to be deemed a "good child."

Good Children: Desirable Children in *Pororo*

Because being good is one of the main concepts emphasized in *Pororo*, this section examines how being good is continually presented through several episodes. In order to do so, it discusses two major concepts which supported being good children: consideration of others and regulating one's self.

Consideration of Others

Many story plots focused on the importance of helpfulness and cooperation. The concept of helping is illustrated in the stories by activities such as sharing with, having interests in, and caring about one's friends—specifically Pororo and his friends. For instance, when Patty (a female penguin) is disappointed about her ability to cook in the story *Robot Cook*, Pororo and the others discuss how they could help her to feel better. When Crong's stuffed animal breaks in *Hello, Friend*, Crong, a little dinosaur, feels sad and upset. Pororo demonstrates that he understands his friend's feeling; he fixes the toy while Crong was sleeps and returns it to him.

Another example is *Red Hat Patty* which is an adaptation of *Little Red Riding Hood*. The characters of the story, Patty and Poby (a big white polar bear), defend three thieves from the police. The thieves initially want to steal

Patty's pie but whenever they attempt to do so they are unsuccessful because of their risk of getting caught. As a result, they lie to Patty and Poby, saying they want to help them. Patty and Poby trust them; they tell the police looking for them that they are "my [their] kind and good friends." This story attempts to encourage young children to see the goodness of others regardless of who they actually are. It also conveys the notion that helping others is important particularly when one is in a difficult situation.

In spite of the *Pororo*'s emphasis on the virtues listed above honesty is not strongly emphasized. Even though Patty and Poby protect the thieves from the police, the thieves do not confess nor do they tell that they intended to steal the pie. They hide behind Poby and indicate how they were scared of the police by their facial expressions. This story indicates that understanding and compassion are more highly valued than other virtues such as honesty. In the last scene of the story everyone looks happy and content—sharing the pie, talking, and smiling. This "happy ending" implies that caring and sharing are crucial in solving any problem—even in reforming criminals. In other words, those acts were seen to overcome conflicts embedded in human relationships. Thus, tolerance is underscored in the story as the first step in creating harmony in a given society—namely, Korea.

The consideration of others is related to the developmental perspective of the importance of friendship and peer relationships during early childhood (Jung, Jung, and Lee 2010). It is also intertwined with the cultural values of Korea, values that emphasize community rather than individuals. A child's acquisition of this concept is essential in Korea, which traditionally highlights the importance of community life and hierarchical relationships between adults and children. This is particularly true since Korean social values spring from a Confucian-based culture in which the common interests of others (community and society) are considered more important than those of any individual. Most Koreans think that children should learn from and respect adults without question; it is children's obligation to accept the rules of a culture. This obligation takes precedence over their own opinions. From this perspective, *Pororo* promotes a critical value of Korean society, consideration of others, as one of the important concepts that young children should learn through their early childhood.

Problem Solving and Cooperation

The characters of the *Pororo* often help friends when a problem is posed to them. However, their collaboration does not always lead them to find a definitive way to solve the problem. Rather, the characters tend to temporarily deal with a problem by seeking an expedient solution. In the previous example, for instance, in order to help Patty, who was disappointed in her own cooking ability, Pororo and his friends think about how to help her and find a solution:

they create a cooking robot for her. They do not consider what cooking procedures she followed, how to improve her cooking ability, or what ingredients were used. Instead of thinking about Patty and her process, they concentrate merely on the result, that is the unsavory cookies. Patty's friends disliked the cookies and their reaction caused Patty's disappointment. As a result, it is necessary for Patty's friends to eliminate the undesirable result by replacing Patty with the robot. In this example the main consideration is how to improve children's final products. It thus implies that outcomes are more important than the process by which the work was done.

This point is also illustrated in *I Can Do, Too.* Harry, a little bird, is criticized over his quantity of work which involved the small amounts of wood and ice he brings along for camping. Nobody in the story discussed or appreciated how much effort he took to do such work. Even though this story had to do with finding Harry's strengths, the characters' work or strengths seem to be evaluated—at least, first—on quantity, not quality.

A character who actually had a problem or created a conflict is not always the one who seeks a solution in the *Pororo.* For instance, when Crong stuffed animal is broken, he is not the one who fixes it. Rather, Pororo does while Crong sleeps. When Patty is disappointed at her own cooking ability, she is not the one who thinks about her ability, but rather her friends. In *Pororo,* friends sympathize with a character who struggles without seeking any help. Their sympathy leads them to ponder on how to solve the problem. They try to solve the problem by working together or often they work on it without that character. On the other hand, a character who causes a problem or a conflict tends to avoid a situation instead of playing an active role in solving it. It is the friends who are charge in of the problem-solving processes. This implies that there will always be "others" who help the children and manage their difficult problems and situations for them. In this process, the children's effort to seek help from others is not required. From this perspective, although *Pororo* attempts to emphasize the importance of cooperation, help, and teamwork, it conveys another message: that a child is not encouraged to be independent or to solve a problem alone. Rather, *Pororo* promotes the notion that she should learn how to rely on others as well as how to be one of the others to be relied upon.

In Korean society, reliability is a key trait. Many educators and adults are concerned about contemporary structures of family which have changed due to such social issues as job loss of a parent and divorce in Korean society (Kim and Cho 2002). In addition, modern technology has been seen to result in changes in the way in which people interact and communicate (Kim 2003; Kim and Cho 2002). Thus, these factors have been considered a main source of the lack of close familial and social relationships in Korea. Such different structures of the family and interactions are seen to cause a negative impact on children's development of self, trust, sociality, and emotion (Kim 2003). Current Korean society emphasizes the values of consideration and helpfulness; these are recurrent themes in *Pororo*. For example, the latest version of the Korean Early Childhood Education Curriculum in 2007 explicitly demonstrated this concept. In the document, the concept of understanding others was regarded as essential for young children to be democratic citizens (Ministry of Education, Science and Technology 2007).

As a result, a child's ability to understand others in *Pororo* is not merely represented as a crucial characteristic to be a good child and to become well-rounded human being. It is also related to Korean social needs, i.e. raising its offspring to be cooperative and able to live in the community successfully without making Korean society disharmonized or disordered. This echoes earlier what Cunningham (1995) and Woodhead (1997) asserted: a good childhood mostly depends on adult lives and social orders. In this way, *Pororo* endorses Korean social values, needs, or expectations regarding childhood.

Self-Regulation

In Korean society, good children exercise self-control. *Pororo* encourages children to regulate their feelings and to take personal responsibility for their actions. For instance, in *Be Careful, Crong!* each lesson that Crong learns centers on what he should not do, not what he should or could do. *Pororo* also perpetuates the notion that children should develop and maintain good habits. Establishing good habits is considered to be each child's own responsibility. For instance, Pororo and Crong do not go to bed even when it was 11P.M. because they were playing. As a result, they got up late, they were late at the meeting with their friends, and had no fun at their friend's house because they fell asleep.

This view reflects the developmental perspective of young children's egocentric characteristics. *Pororo* suggests that children be careful reacting and behaving by highlighting the consequences of bad behavior. This perspective clearly appears in another story, *Pororo and the Magic Flute*. After tricking their friends, Pororo and Crong regret their behavior and apologize to them. However, Pororo and Crong did not fully realize the effect of their prank until their friends play the same trick on them. As a result, they experience the same feelings that their friends did. From this standpoint, their reflection and apology did not result from their own consideration of others. Instead, the reflection and apology occurred because they experienced the negative consequence to their behaviors. According to *Pororo*, thus, a child learns through negative consequences as is appropriate to their developmental characteristic: egocentrism.

The undesirable consequences of bad behavior on the lives of others and on the community is presented is the *Pororo* series. For example, in *Be Careful, Crong!* Crong's mischievous and careless behaviors occur in several locales (a house, a market street, a toy store, and a restaurant) and result in a car accident. In the illustrations, many other people—particularly adults—explicitly show their discomfort with Crong's actions through their facial expressions.

When an undesirable behavior is presented in *Pororo*, the characters do not discuss why they take certain actions. By demonstrating only what they did without appropriate explanation about the reason for their behaviors, *Pororo* often shows only the connection between behaviors and the ensuing consequences; the intentions, needs, desires, and interests that drive the behavior are not considered. Without children's realization of why their intentions or needs are inappropriate or how they can express those in a different way, only a negative association between oneself and others is likely to occur in them. In the mechanism of consequence of *Pororo*, such reasoning is significantly absent: nobody listens or shares with regard to the reasons for the behaviors. As a result, *Pororo* contains a message that bad behavior has bad consequences despite a child's intention or good will.

In this way, *Pororo* advances an image of good children that can be related to the aforementioned notion of childhood as ignorant and presocial and therefore regulated and monitored by adults or society (Archard 1993; James and Prout 1997). Like many other countries, a Korean child is expected to acquire normative behaviors to maintain society and its order in the *Pororo*.

Feelings

An emphasis on self-regulation is also prominent in *Pororo*. The *Pororo* series rarely portrays a character who explicitly expresses his or her feelings. Since the characters do not share their feeling, other characters usually intuit what one is feeling by his or her facial expression. For instance, when Crong accidently breaks his toy monkey, he does not talk about how sad he feels to Pororo. Pororo, sitting next to him, carefully reads Crong's mood based on his facial expression and bases his understanding on that. In *I Want to Fly*, this reserved feeling is also shown. Pororo is frustrated that he could not fly in spite of several trials but he does not verbalize how he feels to his friends. After reading his expression, his friends try to help him even though Pororo does not ask for help. A friend, Eddy (a boy fox) for example, invents an airplane for him. This lack of expressing one's feeling is also portrayed in a different story, *Pororo and Robot Cook*. When Patty is discouraged by her cooking failure, she does not share her feelings. Her friends observe her and spontaneously respond to her need.

The characters' own expressions of feeling, such as "I am happy," "I am sad," and "I am disappointed," are therefore difficult to find in the *Pororo* series. In particular, the characters do not say "thank you" and "sorry" much to the others. As the characters' feelings and difficulties are mostly assumed by the others without clear verbal clarification, *Pororo* conveys another hidden meaning of social assumptions for young children: one's feeling should be well restrained until acknowledged by the others. In addition, because a person's feelings are subject to conjecture, there is no need to express his/her appreciation or regret to others; others know and understand appropriately how the person feels without verbal confirmation. As a result, an individual's feeling can be regarded as transmittable empathetically.

This represents a signigicant Korean cultural value—behaving in a reserved way. Koreans view a person who expresses one's feeling as shallow. Such behavior indicates that the person is governed and controlled by emotions, not logical thinking. Furthermore, expressing a feeling is often considered selfish and immature in that it is focused on the self instead of others and their feelings. On the other hand, a person should be expected to read carefully and should also keenly observe the others' countenance and mood without asking them for direct confirmation. This expectation about observing people's behaviors and feelings—often called "noon-chi (눈치)"—starts to develop in Korean children's very early years. Hence, the issues of a person's feelings in *Pororo* represents this cultural expectation.

From this standpoint, *Pororo* encourages what it means to be a good child by mirroring what Korean society looks for in its children. A good child is one who deals with his or her own emotions and the emotions of others in a way that it is considered appropriate and desirable in the socio-cultural context of Korea. Although many other societies emphasize children's regulation during the early childhood period, each society can have a different purpose of encouraging self-regulation to children. In this case, self-regulation is valued in several Western societies as an important development achievement for children. However, it is critical that a Korean child should learn this concept considering its importance in the fabric of Korean society, the value of common good is emphasized more than many others, as *Pororo* clearly demonstrates.

Conclusion

This chapter discussed the Korean popular educational picture book series *Pororo*, and its way of representing images of young children and early childhood and the way the series portrays the characteristics deemed necessary for "good" Korean children. *Pororo* promotes consideration for others and self-regulation as two such major characteristics. The underlying message is that a happy and healthy community is achieved by helping others through problem solving and self-control. These characteristics are also entangled with the socio-cultural values, expectations, and beliefs that Korean society has for young children. Understanding others and placing others before self are reoccurring themes throughout the *Pororo* stories.

As discussed earlier in this chapter, the popular picture book series purposefully avoids any adult authority figures. No adult forces children to learn a specific value (Cha 2011). By manifesting friendship and play among the characters, *Pororo* underscores young children's own process of problem